Reconstructing Prayer

Reconstructing Prayer

Beyond Deconstructing Your Faith

ANDREW RAY WILLIAMS

Foreword by A. J. Swoboda

CASCADE *Books* • Eugene, Oregon

RECONSTRUCTING PRAYER
Beyond Deconstructing Your Faith

Copyright © 2023 Andrew Ray Williams. All rights reserved. Except for brief quotations in critical publications or reviews, no part of this book may be reproduced in any manner without prior written permission from the publisher. Write: Permissions, Wipf and Stock Publishers, 199 W. 8th Ave., Suite 3, Eugene, OR 97401.

Cascade Books
An Imprint of Wipf and Stock Publishers
199 W. 8th Ave., Suite 3
Eugene, OR 97401

www.wipfandstock.com

PAPERBACK ISBN: 978-1-6667-3824-7
HARDCOVER ISBN: 978-1-6667-9868-5
EBOOK ISBN: 978-1-6667-9869-2

Cataloguing-in-Publication data:

Names: Williams, Andrew Ray, author. | Swoboda, A. J., foreword writer.

Title: Reconstructing prayer : beyond deconstructing your faith / Andrew Ray Williams; foreword by A. J. Swoboda.

Description: Eugene, OR: Cascade Books, 2023 | Includes bibliographical references.

Identifiers: ISBN 978-1-6667-3824-7 (paperback) | ISBN 978-1-6667-9868-5 (hardcover) | ISBN 978-1-6667-9869-2 (ebook)

Subjects: LCSH: Prayer—Christianity. | Theology, Doctrinal—Popular works.

Classification: BV210.2 .W495 2023 (print) | BV210 (ebook)

APRIL 26, 2023 11:33 AM

Scripture quotations are from New Revised Standard Version Bible, copyright © 1989 National Council of the Churches of Christ in the United States of America. Used by permission. All rights reserved worldwide.

To my children—
Adelaide, Audrey, & Anderson

Contents

Foreword by A. J. Swoboda | ix
Acknowledgments | xi
Introduction: Start Here | xiii

1   **God Is Great and Good** | 1
2   **Guests of God** | 13
3   **God and Everything** | 23
4   **Protected by God** | 34
5   **Delivered by God** | 44
6   **Surrounded by God** | 56

Postscript: What Next? | 65

Works Cited | 67

Foreword

For the better part of the last four years, I've given nearly entirely my research and writing attention to the work of understanding what is happening in the hearts and minds of people who are seeking to follow Jesus in the West. In particular my efforts have centered on capturing the heart of what people mean when they say they are "deconstructing" and "doubting" their faith.

What I've found has surprised me. Many, no doubt, do actually intend to mean that they are de*converting* from their faith when they use this language. That is most certainly afoot in many parts of the church of today's world. But more often than not, language of doubt and deconstruction is window dressing for what is really going on.

It's not that many of us are *not* believing in Jesus anymore. It is that we *are* believing in Jesus and it is way harder than we thought it would be. We are, in the words of the apostle, to "work out our salvation with fear and trembling" (Phil 2:2). The trembling is hard. Being shaken is no fun. But it is part of the process. Because of the challenges we face in loving the God that is, we often resort to recreating him in our image. Too often—when we begin to see God in his glory and splendor—we retreat into the safety of worshiping an idol rather than jumping even further into the furious mystery of the God of the universe. All too soon, our vision of Jesus becomes akin to Mr. Potato Head, where we simply adorn him with those things we *want* him to wear.

Foreword

But a god that looks like we want is no God at all. The disciple must love God for who God is, not for who we want him to be.

Dr. Williams has penned an invitation into the furious mystery of prayer where we are beckoned to speak to the God who *is*. This is a short book. But that is what makes it wise. We are told by the wise jester that is behind Ecclesiastes that when we come into the presence of God that it is wise to come with "few words" (Eccl 5:2). Prayer is not the space where we come to rant and lecture God. Prayer is the space of encounter where we come face-to-face with the God who was there before we were. As such, in its simplicity yet profundity, this book reflects a posture of humility.

To the end of learning the sacred art of prayer, the reader would be wise not only to hear the words of Williams the teacher—but also hear the words of those he presents to us. As a scholar and a researcher, he is drawing out some of the generative voices in Christian history to be our teachers. Hear Williams. But also read those whom he brings to the table. For it is there, in the history of the Spirit, where we are taught how the King welcomes us into his presence.

Dr. A. J. Swoboda
Associate Professor of Bible and Theology, Bushnell University
Fall 2022

Acknowledgments

I REALIZE that the opportunity to write this book is a result of the kindness and support of others. So, I wish to personally thank the following people for their contributions to this book. Thanks to my friend Dr. Rick Wadholm Jr. for his constructive feedback on early drafts of these chapters. Of course, any deficiencies remain completely my responsibility. I also want to thank my father, Pastor Brandon Williams, for providing the helpful reflection/discussion questions at the conclusion of each chapter, which in my view add immense value to the book. As always, I am beyond grateful for my wife, Anna, not only for her endless support, but for providing me the time to write. Finally, I am grateful to my amazing children for their inspiration—Adelaide, Audrey, and Anderson. This work is dedicated to the three of you.

Introduction
Start Here

It is hard to remember a time when I did not know Jesus. I grew up in a Christian home, went to church multiple times a week, and attended a Christian school. The Christian faith has always been a part of my life. However, this is not to say that I have never questioned or doubted my faith. Quite the opposite, in fact.

At one point in my life, I experienced a prolonged season of questioning in which I scrutinized many of my own Christian beliefs. While I cannot say that I ever doubted the reality of God or Jesus' divinity, for instance, I did seriously interrogate many, if not most, of my own inherited ideas about God, the church, and the world.

And all of this took place while I was in pastoral ministry.

More than anything, my questioning centered around some of the topics that I will be discussing in this book—how to see God as great and good considering the existence of evil and suffering in the world (chapter 1), how to be assured that I truly was "saved" in any real sense (chapter 2), how science interfaced with the Christian faith (chapter 3), what to make of the afterlife and otherworldly beings such as angels (chapter 4) and demons (chapter 5), how to understand the relationship between the so-called "secular" and the "sacred" aspects of life (chapter 6), among many others. Undoubtedly, some Christians today are wrestling with topics left unexplored here. But, as I have learned, no journey of questioning—or "deconstruction"—is exactly the same.

Introduction

This term, *deconstruction*, is a loaded one. But to define in its broadest terms, deconstruction is the disassembling of something that was once constructed. Theological deconstruction, then, is the disassembling of some part of one's established beliefs. Among Christians, as theologian and pastor A. J. Swoboda has put it, "deconstruction is the new norm." Over half of young people raised in the church deconstruct their faith after high school.

The result is that many people never return to the church. In his poem, "One Sunday," contemporary poet and writer Kip Knott voices such a journey:

> I used to count myself among the sinners. I would
> join them every Sunday in a cave-like cathedral
>
> and chant demands for absolution
> like a sleeper cell waiting for the word.
>
> Once activated, we would rise up and strike down
> any unsuspecting enemy with our testimony.
>
> Secretly, though, each of us was ready to sell out
> the other for the simple promise of salvation.
>
> In the end, it only took one Sunday to accept
> that Sunday was just another day of the week,
>
> one Sunday when I awoke to sound
> of a lone Junco, its beak battered and bloody,
>
> attacking its own reflection in my bedroom window.

For some—such as the speaker in Knott's poem—theological deconstruction leads to a demolished faith. However, my own journey of deconstruction did not end up this way. It did not lead me to abandon my faith. Instead, I found my faith in Jesus strengthened and refined. However, this is not to say that my journey was simple or straightforward. In actuality, it was quite painful, disillusioning, confusing, and anxiety-ridden. Nevertheless, in

INTRODUCTION

the end, I came out with a more robust devotion and affection for Jesus than I had before.

A few factors influenced this outcome. First was my wife's love and perseverance. Anna has always been my closest and most patient confidant and listener. She was understanding and affirming when she needed to be, and she was also wise enough to push back on my cynicism when absolutely necessary. Further, her example of faithfulness to Jesus despite the overwhelming difficulties in her own life has always been extraordinarily inspiring.

Second, I was deeply rooted in the local church. No matter what questions I was wrestling with at the time, I was regularly worshiping with and caring for ordinary Christians whose simple devotion to Jesus was nothing less than God's gift to me. Their simplicity of trust in Jesus was the inspiration I needed in my own times of distress.

Finally, I was studying theology at the graduate and postgraduate levels during this time. So, not only was I deconstructing old ideas, but I was simultaneously being introduced to new, faithful ones that helped me *reconstruct* a more true, good, and beautiful view of God and the world. In the end, I became more rooted in the historic Christian faith, leaving old ideas behind that had more to do with cultural American Christianity than anything else.

Because of these factors, among others, I was able to come out on the other side of my questioning with a renewed commitment to Christ. But as one might expect, these intellectual adjustments impacted my spirituality in profound ways, too. I learned that one's theology is always inseparably related to their spirituality. Another way of saying this is that I discovered that the way I think about God profoundly impacts the way I live with and for God. So, as some of my ideas about God shifted, I found that my spirituality also began to shift. In my opinion, these shifts were for the better. However, they were not always simple or comfortable. I share American Anglican-Pentecostal theologian Chris Green's sentiments when he states:

> I was raised to think of God in specific terms and expect God to act in particular ways. Now, most if not all of

INTRODUCTION

those terms and ways are lost on me. But only because God always proves to be more than those concepts and expectations can handle. Even if I am not always pleased to find this happening to me, I am happy that God is beyond all I ask or think.

As these shifts were taking place in me, I found myself needing to discover how to communicate with God more faithfully. Still, this proved to be difficult—especially at first.

*

According to English revivalist and pastor John Wesley, prayer "is the grand means of drawing near to God." Prayer is one of the primary ways in which we can connect with God. But for those who have gone through a season of doubt or questioning, it is easy to become skeptical or disillusioned about prayer. This can be especially acute for those coming from an evangelical background since within this tradition the term "prayer" is usually analogous to "petitionary prayer." As such, prayers of adoration, contemplation, meditation, and confession are often neglected. So, at least in my case, prayer became difficult when I began to recognize that most of my early prayer life was marked by what spiritual writer Richard Foster has referred to as "egocentric demands."

Since that time I have found that I was not alone. In my experience as a Christian pastor and theology professor, I find that many Christians grapple with prayer. Over time I have come to believe much of this has to do with our misconstrued perceptions about the nature of prayer. By and large, Christians often think of prayer as something we do at certain times and not others. Prayer, then, becomes an add-on to our already busy lives. This paired with what we deem to be our long list of "unanswered prayers" adds to our frustration with the practice.

I believe Brother Lawrence (1611–1691), a lay brother in the Discalced Carmelite order in Paris, can offer us a more faithful way of understanding prayer. For Brother Lawrence, prayer is a "habitual sense of God's presence." Rather than limiting prayer to focused times of petition or intercession, Brother Lawrence believed prayer to be a daily regime of practicing the presence of God. In his mind, it is an ongoing, "habitual, silent, and secret conversation of the soul with God." Prayer, then, is a constant awareness of God and a continuing conversation with God amid one's daily activities.

Therefore, prayer is not simply something we do merely here and there. Rather, prayer is something we are invited to live in moment by moment. Yes, intentional times of focused prayer are necessary and important. However, these focused times must be understood to be within the context of what South African minister and author Andrew Murray has called "living a prayerful life." As Brother Lawrence puts it, "as for my set hours of prayer, they are only a continuation of the same exercise."

When I needed it, Brother Lawrence helped me reenvision a renewed prayer life. After reading his work, I realized that the trouble I had with prayer is that I had an excessively narrow view of it! I also recognized that I had mistakenly thought of prayer as something that is done with the "heart" while my time studying theological ideas was something that was done with the "head." However, when I began to see prayer in more comprehensive and livable terms, I was better able to reintegrate my head and heart. I was able to see prayer and theology as inextricably connected. I now understand what the Christian monk and ascetic Evagrius Ponticus meant when he declared that the "one who prays truly will be a theologian, and one who is a theologian will pray truly."

*

Since I know that I am not the only one who has struggled with living a prayerful life following theological deconstruction, my hope is that this book can help others find their way. What deconstruction tends to pull apart, reconstruction seeks to bring back together, but in (re)new(ed) ways. My desire is to provide a vision of how one might begin reintegrating their head and heart—their theology and spirituality. To fulfill that aim, I have provided a series of theological and devotional reflections on prayerful living.

My desire is that these meditations can serve as examples of reconstructive theology/spirituality.

Perhaps, though, I should say a few words about what this book is *not*. First and foremost, it is not my intent to deliver an explicit "how-to" on theological reconstruction. Since deconstruction tends to be more "caught than taught," I suppose the same may be true for reconstruction. By offering examples of reconstructed theology/spirituality through my meditations, I trust that my reader will be able to discern an outline for their own theological reconstruction. Instead of offering tightly formulated arguments, I have instead provided theological/spiritual reflections and meditations that are aimed towards offering new angles and perspectives on difficult issues that sometimes arise in the Christian life. I do not see these meditations as the final word on any topic, but instead personal reflections on where I believe the Spirit has led me in my own wrestling.

So, this book is *not* an exercise in apologetics. I am not seeking to persuade the skeptic or critic of Christian ideas. Instead, this book is an exercise in what twentieth-century theologian Emil Brunner calls "believing-thinking." My intention is to exhort Christians toward deeper meditation and reflection. I assume, then, that my reader is working with at least an element of faith, including Christians who may be wrestling with doubt, considering that true faith sometimes involves doubt (Mark 9:24). As the German Reformed theologian Jürgen Moltmann has put it, "Profound faith grows up out of the pains and doubts, the torments, and the rebellions."

I also suppose that faithful reconstruction requires dependence upon God. In Scripture, spiritual growth includes moving on from infancy into maturity, *while also* shifting from adulthood into childhood. In biblical terms, it requires moving on from "milk" to "solid food" (Heb 5:12–14), while concurrently becoming less "adultlike" and more "childlike" (Matt 18:3). The apostle Paul is right: at times, the gospel can sound like utter foolishness (1 Cor 1:18)! And yet, as we follow God into this gospel paradox,

INTRODUCTION

we will soon recognize that "God's foolishness is wiser than human wisdom" (1 Cor 1:25).

All of this leads me to believe that developing a reconstructed account of prayer is marked by *mature dependence*.

Suitably, then, I will be structuring my reflections around common children's prayers. In each chapter I will be focusing on the themes implicitly and explicitly stated in a children's prayer, reflecting theologically and devotionally on it in hopes that God will renew both intellect and hearts. By offering meditations on the words of children, I am hoping that the reader will take up childlike prayers as acts of faith and see how this might open new ways of understanding specific issues related to Christian faith. These meditations are meant to be invitational—welcoming people to prayerfully grapple and reflect. As such, this book calls for a more paced and reflective reading.

In sum, I hope that this book will aid others in thinking more carefully about how the mind and the heart can, and should, cooperate in the Christian life. And I pray that, in Jesus' words, those reading these words will find themselves loving God with all their heart, soul, strength, and mind, enabling them to love their neighbor as themselves (Luke 10:27).

1

God Is Great and Good

God is great and God is good,
Let us thank him for our food;
By his blessings, we are fed,
Give us, Lord, our daily bread.
Amen.

I GREW up Pentecostal.
This means, among other things, that I grew up imagining that God could do anything. From an early age, I heard stories concerning God performing miraculous deeds of power. I became acquainted with the Old Testament narratives that recounted God creating the cosmos, dividing the Red Sea, speaking through Balaam's donkey, and sending fire down from heaven in response to Elijah's prayer, along with many others. Of course, I was also taught about Jesus healing the sick, freeing the demon-possessed, and raising the dead. But in my church, God was not done with doing extraordinary works. Hebrews 13:8 was painted on the back wall of our sanctuary: "Jesus Christ is the same yesterday and today and forever."

And while God's greatness was a central theme in my Christian upbringing, equally important was God's goodness.

The message was plain: "God is love" (1 John 4:8). I was fortunate enough to have been directed towards envisioning God as the father in Jesus' story of the prodigal son, who was all-loving, forgiving, and compassionate. But he was not simply good in the abstract. Jesus, the Good Shepherd, cared for *me*. The Holy Spirit was *my* comforter—*my* advocate. In short, I grew up with a warm doctrine of God. God was almighty, but also compassionate and kind. My faith was also an affective one—one that sought to know the greatness and goodness of God, not only cognitively but also experientially.

However, as I continued to follow God into my college years, I began struggling to comprehend how God's greatness and goodness flowed together. It was during this time that I began reflecting more deeply on the disappointments I had with God. My older brother Timothy, for instance, had lived—and still does live—with cerebral palsy and mental disability. Around this time, my younger brother Nathan was diagnosed with ulcerative colitis, causing him to suffer significantly on a day-to-day basis. During those years, I also traveled to Central America, witnessing the most profound poverty I had ever encountered.

Over time, I began growing more skeptical about how God could be both great and good in the presence of actual senseless suffering and difficulty. I started wondering that if God is all-powerful and all good, why do I see such pain and suffering?

Bart Ehrman, James A. Gray Distinguished Professor of Religious Studies at the University of North Carolina, in his book *God's Problem*, shares his reasoning for abandoning his evangelical faith and adopting modern atheism:

> The problem of suffering has haunted me for a very long time. It was what made me begin to think about religion when I was young, and it was what led me to question my faith when I was older. Ultimately, it was the reason I lost my faith.

Ehrman is not alone. Others have cited what has become known as "the problem of evil" for abandoning their Christian faith. This issue is mentioned among skeptics so often it has sometimes been called the "rock of atheism."

Still, other notable evangelical Christians have given varied reasons. For example, Hillsong worship leader Marty Sampson surprised his Instagram followers when he first publicly shared that he had been in the process of "losing his faith." Sampson, who has written Christian worship songs that have been sung all around the world, such as "Better Than Life," "For Who You Are," "Carry Me," and "O Praise the Name (Anástasis)," stated that he was giving up his belief in God because of all the issues "no one talks about" in the church:

> How many miracles happen. Not many. No one talks about it. Why is the Bible full of contradictions? No one talks about it. How can God be love yet send four billion people to a place, all coz they don't believe? No one talks about it.

Sampson is not alone. In the age of the internet, these deconversion stories have and are growing in popularity. Others cite similar reasons for abandoning their Christian faith. And according to Sampson, "no one" is talking about these critical, significant issues. But is this true? Is no one talking about these crucial issues?

Fortunately for Christians everywhere, Marty Sampson is mistaken.

Much to my surprise, when I arrived at seminary, I learned that Christians had been discussing such issues for over two millennia. Not only were contemporary Christian apologists debating the "new atheists" on YouTube, but many of the early voices within Christian history had been defending their faith in light of real hostility.

When it came to the question of theodicy (the "defense of God" in light of the existence of evil), I learned about ways Christians have wrestled with this question for thousands of years. Though I was introduced to early Christian approaches, I became more acquainted with the way recent conversations among Christian theologians were developing in seeking to "answer" such a problem. However, I was often left dissatisfied with various "schools of thought" since, in my view, they too often focused either on God's greatness or God's goodness, one at the expense of the other.

For instance, in seeking to answer the "problem of evil" some Christian thinkers emphasize that God is great—almighty, powerful, and glorious—and yet either determines or causes evil, in the end sacrificing God's goodness. However, others tend to elevate God's goodness by emphasizing his suffering, empathy, and care, but to the extent of making God essentially weak, unable to do much of anything to overcome evil. It seemed to me—and still does in fact—that we must say that God is both perfectly great and perfectly good, and not one at the expense of the other. This conviction stems from the fact that the church must seek to speak as Scripture speaks. But during this formative time, I still had difficulty making sense of *how* to make Scripture's claim my own.

As I began pastoring, I realized that this question had great practical relevance, not only for my life but for those whom I was shepherding. I have since recognized that this question surfaces quite often in people's lives, whether one explicitly voices it or not. If they have not already, most Christians at some point will begin asking, "Where was God?" "Where was God when I was abandoned by my spouse?" "Where was God when I suffered at the hands of my abuser?" "Where was God when my loved one died of cancer?" The questions surrounding innocent suffering are ones that both Christians and non-Christians alike face.

And yet, even today, Christian children are taught to pray that "God is great, *and* God is good."

The question becomes for us Christians—how can we move on from either/or?

*

How can we honestly pray that God is both great and good?

An ancient Hebrew poet found a way. Psalm 100 is a poem of thanksgiving, thanking the God of Israel for both his greatness and goodness:

> Make a joyful noise to the LORD, all the earth.
> Worship the LORD with gladness;
> come into his presence with singing.
> Know that the LORD is God.
> It is he that made us, and we are his;
> we are his people, and the sheep of his pasture.
> Enter his gates with thanksgiving,
> and his courts with praise.
> Give thanks to him, bless his name.
> For the LORD is good;
> his steadfast love endures forever,
> and his faithfulness to all generations.

For the poet, God is both the sovereign Creator and the loving, faithful Sustainer. He is the initiator and upholder. And for the poet, it is because of God's greatness and goodness that one can ascribe such glory and perfection to God. Because of God's nature and character, one can rejoice in thanksgiving. Unlike the other gods surrounding Israel, the God of Israel was both great and good.

Yet, this is not to say that this poet has necessarily been sheltered from suffering and disappointment. The poet was part of a community and tradition that also wrote numerous songs of lament. In Psalm 77, for instance, the poet cries out:

> Will the LORD spurn forever,
> and never again be favorable?
> Has his steadfast love ceased forever?
> Are his promises at an end for all time?
> Has God forgotten to be gracious?
> Has he in anger shut up his compassion?

Despite the poet's questioning, he does not feel so far removed that he cannot speak to God. While speaking of God, make no mistake—the poet is talking *to* God *about* God. Unlike most of us, the psalmists seemed to feel comfortable expressing both praise and anguish to God *in faith*. The psalmists were able to trust in God despite their disillusionment. Still, the psalmists often had questions for God. Appeals to God make up nearly half of the

Psalms. Perhaps the most shocking of all the Psalms is Psalm 88. It is unyieldingly dark. It is the only one of the lament psalms that does not transform into praise.

In short, these biblical poems provide the possibility of having what Welsh poet and Anglican priest R. S. Thomas calls "linguistic confrontation(s) with ultimate reality."

During my times of searching, these "lament" psalms have served as a great comfort to me, as well as the biblical figure, Job. He was a man who struggled and suffered and discovered that life is often enveloped in mystery and unintelligibility. Though Job never gave up faith in God, he did question God. Job shows us that oftentimes, the only lucid thing to do is to question. One could make a case that God approved of Job's questions more than he approved of the superficial answers of Job's "friends."

Eastern Orthodox theologian Vladimir Lossky rightly points out that God justifies Job, who contended with God, while God's wrath was kindled against Job's friends, who spoke in favor of God determining evil. In the end, God speaks and says, "You have not spoken of me what is right, as my servant Job has" (Job 42:7). Job realizes the vastness of the cosmic catastrophe brought about through Satan and human rebellion. The truth of the matter is that often when faced with difficulty, the only faithful thing to do is to cry out in questioning.

Christian apologists continue to argue the issues contained with the problem of evil. However, as of late, I have realized that those questions—which are undoubtedly important—are perhaps *not* the most important questions we must address. Scripture is far less interested in conjecture on the origin of evil than in opposition to it in the belief of ultimate triumph in Jesus Christ. And even if we did have an obvious answer to the problem of evil and suffering, in my experience personally and pastorally, this "problem" weighs more heavily on the "heart" than on the "mind."

Often, the problem is *not* that we don't have a clear answer to this difficulty, but that we have not been trained in wisdom on how to navigate complex territory with God.

God Is Great and Good

*

On August 21, 2017, the "Great American Solar Eclipse" made a 185-mile-wide shadow across the continental United States. Many news outlets reported on the event, encouraging viewers to observe this rare happening. However, to view the eclipse, one needed to purchase protective eyewear, since looking at the eclipse with the naked eye could cause significant damage to a person's vision.

Similarly, too many of us have looked at the suffering around us without the defensive lens of God's goodness *and* greatness to help us make sense of what we are viewing. As a result, some have lived with lasting damage to their vision of God's character, stunting or even demolishing their journey with God. The truth is that sometimes suffering can blind us to God's true nature. To make sense of difficulty, we can easily pervert our view of God. Often to console ourselves and others, we claim that there must be some ultimate meaning or purpose in our misery.

But this must be false—God is not—and cannot—be the author of evil. Christianity is a religion of salvation! Our Christian faith is in a God who has come to rescue his creation and people from the farce of sin and the emptiness of death. Thus, we should never sacrifice God's goodness by attributing evil to God. We must also avoid the equal danger of suggesting that God cannot prevent and conquer evil. We must recall that God is both good *and* great.

In prayer, we do not skirt demanding situations and avoid challenging questions. Instead, we trust and hope in God amid the difficulty. And if we must, we can echo the cry of the desperate father of the demon-possessed boy "I believe; help my unbelief!" (Mark 9:24). This is a turn toward Jesus, as everything within us urges us to turn away from him. Implicit within this biblical cry is the notion that our ability to believe in Christ is a gift from him. Faith and belief are impossible to obtain without Christ. This is a good reminder for those of us who often feel as if our faith depends upon our own will. The apostle Paul would balk at such a suggestion! As he said to the believers in Ephesus: "For by grace you have been saved through faith, and this is not your own doing; it is the gift of God" (Eph 2:8).

But to echo that biblical cry—"I believe; help my unbelief"—we need to debunk the false idea that doubt, in and of itself, is inherently sinful.

As we have already shown, *faithful doubt* is prevalent throughout Scripture. And crucial to understanding doubt is appreciating that it is only possible as a point of transition. The Swiss theologian Emil Brunner is right in pointing out that doubt either becomes faith or unbelief. Who or what one turns to determines what doubt ends up becoming. Faithful doubt—as opposed to unfaithful doubt—is the kind of questioning expressed *to* God rather than in isolation *from* God. As the Psalms often show us, what begins as doubt can be faithfully transformed into hope!

And this Christian hope is the promise of a new creation brought about by God's greatness. For the Christian, it is the hope for a different world that makes us incapable of accepting the brokenness of this world. Without a vision for true life, we would not recognize what marks a false life.

What I am claiming is this: hope is the only way to make sense of suffering. Yet, without suffering, we would have no hope. Through Christ's suffering, hope was born. On the cross, Jesus protested against the state of this world. Because of his protest, we can envision the world as it should be and one day will be. As American writer William Faulkner once observed: "What's wrong with this world is, it's not finished yet."

In the meantime, we are to weep with those who weep and rejoice with those who rejoice. God, too, joins in this weeping and rejoicing. As the "theologian of hope" Jürgen Moltmann puts it, "God weeps with us so that we may one day laugh with him."

All of this means that we can trust in God's goodness through difficulty while also trusting in his greatness to overcome it. With God, we can hate evil "with a perfect hatred" (Ps 139:22) while concurrently anticipating God's intention and capacity to destroy evil finally. In other words, the real solution to the problem of all misery is redemption.

God Is Great and Good

*

Our children's prayer offers us the language to probe the relation between God's identity and human thankfulness. This prayer assumes a connection of some kind: "God is great, and God is good . . . Let us thank him."

Perhaps the association lies in the fact that a proper understanding of God ought to naturally lead us towards gratitude. John Cassian, a fifth-century Christian monk, once stated that "thanksgiving" is "born of the consideration of God's blessings and His greatness and goodness." Put another way, praying "God is great, and God is good" is preparatory for praying our next line: "Let us thank him for our food." Cassian is right to point out that prayers of thanksgiving genuinely arise when one contemplates God's true beauty.

I have often wondered whether Christians would live fuller lives of gratitude if they better understood the God we worship. The way we view God impacts the way we live. So often we live lives marked by discontentment and feelings of lack. However, through prayer, we can get outside of ourselves and contemplate the God who has gifted us with more than we can even perceive. The spiritual writer Henri Nouwen rightly stated that "the closer we come to God in prayer, the more we become aware of the abundance of God's gifts to us." Nouwen is exactly right—and curiously enough, this concept is implicit within the prayer we are reflecting on. Once we recognize how genuinely great and good God is, we naturally move into a prayerful gratitude.

And once we can see the world through the lens of gratitude, we recognize that life in all its manifestations is a gift from God. We may even realize the presence of these gifts amid our pains and disappointments. What once seemed like a hindrance to our spiritual lives turned out to be a gift, not because God is causing difficulty—certainly not!—but because through these twists and turns, we can find ourselves more deeply rooted in Christ. Therefore, according to Nouwen, gratitude can become a quality of our hearts "that allows us to live joyfully and peacefully even though our struggles continue."

As we raise our two daughters, my wife and I remind them to express thanks once they receive a gift. We have discovered that it is often the natural inclination of a child to run off and begin enjoying a gift immediately once it is received. However, early lessons in gratitude must stress the importance of genuine, heartfelt, intentional thanks. Still, some of us never outgrow this tendency in our spiritual lives. We must recognize that, as the prayer goes, "by his blessings, we are fed." As James 1:17 says, "every perfect gift is from above, coming down from the Father." And in response, we "give thanks" for such blessings (1 Thess 5:18).

But this is not to say that God somehow needs our gratitude. God is not needy but already fulfilled. Out of that fulfillment he gives to those who are in need—us. He died for us while we were still sinners (Rom 5:8). The truth of the matter is that gratitude benefits us. It orients us toward God in a way that we can recognize and enjoy the gifts he seeks to bestow.

Thomas Merton, the prolific Trappist monk, states it this way:

> To be grateful is to recognize the love of God in everything He has given us—and He has given us everything. Every breath we draw is a gift of His love, every moment of existence is grace, for it brings with us immense graces from Him. Gratitude, therefore, takes nothing for granted, is never unresponsive, is constantly awakening to new wonder, and is to praise the goodness of God. For the grateful person knows that God is good, not by hearsay but by experience. And that is what makes all the difference.

*

First featured in Jesus' own prayer life, the next line—"Give Us Lord, Our Daily Bread"—has been recited in churches for many centuries as a part of the *Our Father*. Still, I wonder if most Christians who pray this prayer have reflected deeply upon it?

When doing so, we would be wise to remember that Jesus warns his disciples not to heap up empty phrases to God, thinking that they will be heard because of their many words (Matt 6:5). Instead, Jesus opts for simple phrases, one of them being, "Give us this day our daily bread" (Matt 6:11). It is a prayer of faith and trust. We should not be surprised, then, that Jesus exhorts his disciples to not worry about tomorrow, for today's trouble is enough for today (Matt 6:34). When we pray for "daily bread," then, we are praying for what we need today, and no more. Implicitly, we confess both that God is the giver of all gifts and that we are reliant and needy creatures. We can trust that just as our heavenly Father dresses the lilies beautifully and provides food for the birds, so too he will provide for his children.

And yet, this does not get to the heart of the whole meaning of "daily bread." In other words, we cannot stop here, thinking this prayer is merely about material needs. Early Christian readers, such as Tertullian, recognized that this also refers to Christ, himself. Jesus is the "bread of life" (John 6:35). And when we seek him first, his kingdom, and his righteousness, God will take care of everything else (Matt 6:33). Therefore, in petitioning for daily bread, we are asking for our concrete needs to be met, but also for our spiritual hunger to be fulfilled.

*

As was stated earlier, Psalm 100 affirms God's greatness and God's goodness. In light of this almighty, loving God, the worshipers are justified in entering "his gate with thanksgiving and his courts with his praise". The worshipers can then trust God, whose "steadfast love endures forever."

I want to contend that we too can join in this praise. We have been invited to share in the same affirmations and offer the same kind of thanksgiving. Considering the ultimate act of redemption brought about through Jesus, Christians now have a fuller perspective on the psalms' themes of divine power, divine love, thanksgiving, and trust. In light of this new perspective, how much more can we be thankful to God for what he has given us in his Son? How much more can we echo these songs of thanksgiving? How much more can we trust God with the difficulty and disillusionment we experience? And how much more can we hope?

Perhaps reading Psalm 100 with new eyes will lead us to pray like children, again.

For Reflection or Discussion

As you pray this children's prayer in light of this chapter, consider reflecting on and/or discussing the following questions:

1. Does your understanding of God lean more toward "God is great" or "God is good"? How do you think this view impacts the way you relate to God?
2. Do you believe God welcomes your questions regarding his seeming lack of involvement in certain circumstances, or are these types of questions "off-limits"? Why?
3. What experiences in your life have caused you to question God's goodness? In reflecting upon this chapter, what can aid you in seeing God more accurately?
4. How would your prayers, conversations, and meditations be different if your "questions were expressed to God rather than in isolation from God"?
5. What does the statement, "hope is the only way to make sense of suffering," mean to you?

2

Guests of God

Come, Lord Jesus, be our guest,
And let this food to us be blessed. Amen.

I STILL remember "inviting" God into my life as a young child. Though I was only five years old, I was serious about giving my life to Jesus—as serious as any five-year-old could be. Years later I was baptized and thus, "fully converted."

However, in my teenage years, I began wondering whether my initial confession was genuine or serious enough. When I found myself in evangelistic settings, my concern was amplified. I wondered: Was my early "decision" naïve? Had I truly believed in God? Had I felt strongly enough about God to make my decision "count"? These questions, among others, plagued me. I was not only confused but at times anguished.

The Christian Reformer Martin Luther, too, spent much of his life without assurance of his standing before God. Reflecting on that period of his life he later stated, "Life had become a living hell." Fortunately for him and us, Luther was eventually able to diagnose the problem leading to this existential uncertainty. He discovered that an overly subjective understanding of authentic

Christian faith causes believers to trust in their feelings more than they trust in God.

It does not help that in our Western society, we have been trained to believe that our subjective awareness is what makes reality *real*. Luther and others from the Christian tradition offer us a needed correction in how we view all of life. In short, these voices invite us to consider that the objective presence of God is what gives reality to all things.

I eventually came to this realization as well. My early view of salvation was excessively subjective and one-sided, causing me to assume that salvation rested on my personal experiences and feelings. I came to appreciate that no one can convert themselves. God alone can do it. This means, then, that I must not trust in my confession in faith, since that is not what saves me. God saves me, so my trust and my faith are in him. I now rest knowing that all it takes is just a small amount of faith—that of a mustard seed, in fact.

*

The anxiety I experienced around my salvation is a symptom of a larger problem within various forms of Christianity. Some of us have been trained to believe that God is responsive to our initiatives. This implies that God is mostly inactive, waiting to be moved to action by our desires and faith. Not only is this biblically and theologically mistaken, but it is also deeply harmful to our spiritualities. In fact, it makes us ultimately responsible for fashioning our own lives.

The opening line of our prayer—"Come, Lord Jesus"—seems to exacerbate this very issue. On the surface, this prayer appears to communicate that God would not come without us welcoming him. We might be tempted to think that when we pray, we are the ones who are inviting God to act. Perhaps we might think that without our petitions, God is passive.

But we would be mistaken.

We first find the phrase "Come, Lord Jesus" in the book of Revelation. In response to Jesus' pronouncement, "Surely I am coming soon", the writer replies, "Amen. Come, Lord Jesus" (22:20). In Revelation, then, "Come, Lord Jesus" is not so much a *request* as it is a *response*.

This underlines a vital truth for our spiritual lives: our invitations to God are *responsive* rather than *initiatory*. This is what Paul argues in Romans 5. God takes the step towards us, and it is not until we are graced that we are able to then respond to God's work in our lives. This means that while our relationship with God is indeed reciprocal, it is never interchangeable. God is indeed relational. But he is the pursuer, and we are the responders.

Now, this does not mean that somehow human effort is useless or unimportant. The liberty that God has granted to us is indeed real and should be welcomed. Our effort *does* factor into God's workings. But we must realize that our cooperation with God is graced. Or to put it another way, we are moved by the Spirit in cooperating with God. The Russian ascetic Bishop Theophanes puts it this way: "The Holy Ghost, acting within us, accomplishes with us our salvation". I think this is exactly what the apostle Paul is getting at when he states that although he worked harder than anyone else, anything good in him must be credited to God's grace—*not* his own effort (1 Cor 15:10), or when he states that he takes hold of that for which Christ took hold of him (Phil 3:12).

John Cassian has provided a helpful agricultural analogy to illustrate this truth. According to Cassian, without proper rainfall and healthy soil, a farmer is unable to produce wholesome crops. Even if a farmer is constantly hard at work in his field, without such work from within the earth, his work is useless. Similarly, our will and strength are futile without God's grace and mercy working within us. Again, our effort *does* matter, but we cannot accomplish anything apart from God's help, since our effort is a simple willingness to cooperate with what God is at work doing. As Cassian puts it, "Just as the divine goodness does not bestow an abundant yield on sluggish farmers who do not plow their field frequently, so neither will night-long anxiety be profitable to those who labor if it has not been smiled upon by the Lord's mercy."

God stimulates the beginnings of good desire and grants us the ability to bring about the things that we rightly wish for. Or in Paul's words: "He who supplies seed to the sower and bread for food will supply and multiply your seed for sowing and increase the harvest of your righteousness" (2 Cor 9:10). For some, this careful balance between God's grace and human activity might seem like splitting hairs, but our early fathers and mothers in the faith knew better. Without careful thought, we end up living in ways that are counter to the gospel. We end up living as if God is dependent upon our effort, rather than our effort being dependent upon him! Andrew Murray puts it well:

> The idea so many Christians have of grace is this: that their conversion and pardon are God's work, but now, in gratitude to God, it is their work to live as Christians and follow Jesus. There is always the thought of a work that has to be done, and even though they pray for help, still the work is theirs. They fail continually and become hopeless; and their despondency only increases their feelings of helplessness. No, wandering one; as it was Jesus who drew you when He said, "Come," so it is Jesus who keeps you when He says, "Abide." The grace to come and the grace to abide are both from Him alone.

Let's face it: we are used to assuming *we* build our own destinies through determination and hard work. Influenced by the attitudes of our age, we fail to recognize that the phrase "pull yourself up by your bootstraps" is not a true theological statement. The central message of the gospel is the exact opposite: without Christ, we are dead in sin and unable to do anything of value. Again, in the words of Murray, "Our doing and working are but the fruit of Christ's work in us."

*

When we stop trusting in our own efforts and instead, trust in God, we finally see our primary relation to God as "guest" rather than "host." This is where our children's prayer needs some significant correction: God is *not* our guest—we are his guests! We are the ones invited. As Jesus says, "Come to me, all you that are weary and are carrying heavy burdens, and I will give you rest" (Matt 11:28). We cannot get this backward: God is the host—we are the guests. He invites us into partaking in his life.

When discussing hospitality, I cannot help but think of my wife, Anna, since she places such a high value on hospitability. Though we have always lived modestly, Anna has continually made our homes inviting and hospitable to others. She has always gone out of her way to show value to others through warm acceptance and inclusion. However, whether she likes it or not, there are natural limits placed upon her hospitality. In our home, space is often limited—and our time is constrained. Yet, this is what makes God's hospitality radically different from our own.

God is not restricted by space or time. His hospitality knows no bounds. To illustrate this, Lutheran theologian Robert Jenson has made the daring claim that God is "roomy." By this, Jenson means that God is the ultimate host who makes room for others. God, then, can invite people into his life without it distorting or compromising his own. Therefore, God is *infinitely* roomy. Jenson is right about this. God can and does open room within himself for us—and he never tires of it, for we can never exhaust his loving embrace.

Jenson recognizes that we see this most supremely in the life of Jesus. Jesus was not a "guest" in this world. Jesus did not come to be a guest, but to be the True Host. Since our ultimate destiny is God, Jesus hosts true life for those who are willing to follow him. He beckons us to union with himself. This union, though, is not only meant for some but all. The message of the gospel is that Jesus came for everyone (John 3:16) and desires all to be saved (1 Tim 2:4).

And those of us who have experienced his rescue have not only been saved *from* something, but also *for* something. We have been saved not only to become beneficiaries of God's hospitality but bringers of it. In other words, we are not taken into God's life merely for our own sake, but also for the sake of hosting God's love in the world. This is what Finnish Lutheran-Pentecostal theologian

Veli-Matti Kärkkäinen means when he states that "hospitality is a Christian virtue, derived from God, who is giver *and* gift." God gifts us with God, so that we may carry the gift of his presence to others.

But what might it look like to host God's love in the world? To put it simply, it looks like Jesus' life. It looks like loving the unlovable, touching the untouchables, and welcoming the stranger. To say it differently, often it appears like partaking in Christ's sufferings (1 Pet 4:13). It means potentially putting ourselves into harm's way. We cannot romanticize hospitality—hospitality carries real risk. True hospitality is turning toward the other, which can often become costly and sacrificial, as we see demonstrated in the life of Jesus. To those on the outside, becoming God's hosts may not look triumphant and victorious. But in the end, it proves to be the power of the gospel.

In one of his Christmas sermons, Dietrich Bonhoeffer—the German pastor-theologian who was martyred by Hitler's Third Reich—captures this truth well. According to Bonhoeffer, God's power looks quite different from how we typically envision it. As we see in both Jesus' birth and his death, God's power is found in what we typically view as weakness.

> God has become a child! Here the child is poor like us, wretched like us, miserable and helpless like us, a human being of flesh and blood like us, our brother. And yet he is God, yet he is might. Where is the divinity, where is the might of this child? In the divine love by which he becomes like us. His misery in the manger is his might. In the power of love he overcomes the chasm between God and humanity, he overcomes sin and death, he forgives sin and raises from death. Kneel down before this wretched manger, before this child of poor parents, and repeat in faith the stammering words of the prophet: "God-Might!"—and he will become your God and strength.

Not only are we to wonder at God's meekness, but we are to bow before it. Becoming hosts in the world means humbling ourselves before God's humility. Postured before God, we then can receive the power of God's love and share it with the world.

Though we come as guests, God makes us into hosts.

*

Jesus liked to eat. As the evangelical scholar Gordon Smith has noted, "It was so much a part of his ministry and his life that one almost gets the sense that when he wasn't preaching and teaching, he was eating." Food was also featured in many of Jesus' teachings and parables, often comparing eating and drinking to the kingdom of God. Jesus demonstrated the kingdom, then, by eating with various kinds of people. In addition to his disciples, Jesus also ate with those on the fringes of society such as outcasts and tax collectors—those like Mary Magdalene and Zacchaeus, whom others disregarded and loathed. As theologian Geoffrey Wainwright has argued, there are clear parallels between the feeding of the crowds in Mark 6 and 8, for instance, and the blessing/thanksgiving, breaking, and distribution in Jesus' Last Supper with his disciples. In other words, we cannot make a clear delineation between the meals Jesus shared with his disciples and those meals he shared with sinners. All meals Jesus shared with others were meals of redemption.

In speaking to his disciples, Jesus predicted a day when he would eat and drink with them "at my table in my kingdom" (Luke 22:30). This sheds light on the fact, as Smith points out, that Jesus viewed his meals as events that anticipated the *marriage supper of the Lamb* at the fulfillment of history (Rev 19:6–9). In eating with sinners and disciples, Jesus signaled that the kingdom was inclusive of all people—no matter their past fortune. Thus, when we pray "let this food to us be blessed," it is imperative we keep the relational and redemptive character of Jesus' meals in mind. His eating and drinking were about forgiving and freeing people.

So it is with us when we gather to take Holy Communion. At Christ's table, we come acknowledging that we have sinned yet again in thought, word, and deed and must appropriate the forgiveness of God, which delivers us from shame and energizes us to operate in the light. During the Last Supper, Jesus took a loaf of bread, blessed it, broke it, and gave it to his disciples. After his instruction to eat "[his] body," he took a cup and said, "Drink from it, all of you for this is my blood of the covenant, which is poured out for the forgiveness of sins" (Matt 26:26–38). Whenever we break bread with Christ and his disciples, we are offered reconciliation.

Holy Communion is the place where forgiveness is both honored and experienced. We eagerly come to the table of mercy to receive once more forgiveness and embrace. Here we quite literally "taste and see that the Lord is good" (Ps 34:8). However, the meal is never only about our own forgiveness. We are also commissioned and energized to forgive others. Holy Communion is communion with God as well as others. We ought to bear in mind that Jesus instructs us to be reconciled with others before bringing our gifts to the altar (Matt 5:23). As the Anglican theologian Rowan Williams has said, "One of the most transformingly surprising things about Holy Communion is that it obliges you to see the person next to you as wanted by God."

Here we discover more of the connection between Jesus' "blessing" of meals and his presence in the world through the church. Eating with Jesus sets our vision aright—it helps us to see one another and the world appropriately. Eastern Orthodox thinker Alexander Schmemann helpfully reminds us that historically the celebration of Holy Communion ends with the celebration of returning to the world. This implies that communion with one another was not the end, but the beginning, since God has made us capable of fulfilling his mission in the world. Or in the words of Rowan Williams, "Jesus is not only someone who exercises hospitality; he draws out hospitality from others. By his welcome, he makes other people capable of welcoming."

In this way, we might become like the apostle Paul—one who received God's hospitality and was then able to share it with others amid great peril (Acts 27:27–42). Finding himself as a prisoner sailing to Rome, Paul was able to host God's peace among frantic sailors. When a fierce storm struck the sea and everyone on board was frenzied, Paul brought about God's peace through a meal. In the middle of the storm, Paul took bread, gave thanks to God, blessed it, shared it, and as a result, all were encouraged. In the end, everyone escaped safely to shore. In the same way, as we learn to accept God's gifts, we are then able to share them with others. Those who accept God's hospitality will find themselves fleeing securely to shore.

Brunner once wrote, "The Church exists by mission, just as a fire exists by burning." A stack of wood is not a fire if the wood is not burning, just as a community is not the church if it is not following Jesus into his mission. He gathers his people to nourish them with himself but then commissions them to share what they have received with the world. He has a purpose for us beyond ourselves.

*

When I first welcomed God into my life those many years ago, whether I realized it or not, I was not taking the lead. I was not inviting God into my life. Instead, I was responding to God's invitation. Though unbeknownst to me at the time, God had been drawing me by his prevenient grace prior to my own awareness. But his hospitality was not extended to me merely for my own good, but the good of the world. God offered it so that I can be remade into one who extends this same hospitality to others.

If we are going to move into maturity in Christ, we must deconstruct the egocentric attitudes that blind us to God's purposes for his hospitality. Or, to put it in biblical terms, we must "repent." Only then can we reconstruct a new way forward that sees ourselves as *responsible* recipients of God's grace. Only then can we see ourselves as children "born again" into a new family, with a new identity and a new mission.

For Reflection or Discussion

As you pray this children's prayer in light of this chapter, consider reflecting on and/or discussing the following questions:

1. At what point in your life did God become more than just an idea to you?
2. Do you believe God was active and at work in your life prior to your confession of faith? Why or why not?
3. When you "invite God" into a situation, how might it help to recognize that God is already working and, rather than *requesting*, you are actually *responding* to God's initiation?
4. Hospitality is somewhat of a lost art in our Western culture. In what ways can you practice hospitality by "loving the unlovable, touching the untouchables, and welcoming the stranger," knowing it will sometimes be costly and require sacrifice?
5. Ponder the statement, "God gifts us with God, so that we may carry the gift of his presence to others." Pause and give thanks for the people who have embodied this truth, thus impacting your life for good.
6. Next time you approach Christ's table, how might realizing that he is the host and you are the guest change your experience of Holy Communion?

3

God and Everything

> *Thank you for the world so sweet.*
> *Thank you for the food we eat.*
> *Thank you for the birds that sing.*
> *Thank you God for everything.*
> *Amen.*

I HAVE seen both the best and worst qualities of Christian education. I have the experience to prove it.

I grew up attending a Christian elementary, middle, and high school, then graduating from a Christian college and later, a Christian seminary. Today, my children attend a Christian elementary school and I teach theology at a few Christian universities. Thus, since I continue to entrust my own time, energy, and children to Christian educational institutions, I believe they have significant strengths and benefits. However, this does *not* mean that I have failed to recognize serious problems that can often accompany them.

In my mind, one obvious issue is how some contemporary Christian educators approach the relationship between the sciences and the Christian faith. From an early age, I was told contemporary scientific developments and my faith were at odds. "Secular science" (as opposed to "Christian science") was a Trojan horse for worldly beliefs. As a result, I was trained as a child to be quite distrustful of scientific advances. I now see, however, that the belief that one must choose between science or faith is deeply flawed.

Our children's prayer rightly upholds the goodness and beauty of God's creation. But as Christians living in a scientific age, our confession cannot stop there. There is a significant need in our day for thoughtful Christians to provide further reflection on how the Christian faith can interact with the modern sciences.

However, at least in some North American evangelical circles, these kinds of pursuits are often burdened by difficulty due to various political, cultural, and theological anxieties.

*

Christian theology has always asserted that creation is a visible, tangible, and endless expression of God's wisdom. As the apostle Paul told the early Christians in Rome, God's eternal power and divine nature can be discerned through everything he has made (Rom 1:20). And as the biblical poet exclaims, "the earth is the Lord's and all that is in it" (Ps 24:1). The world, then, bears the marks of creative ingenuity.

However, with the rise of modern sciences, Christians have become confused about how to reconcile Christian theological convictions with scientific explanations. In my estimation, this is further complicated and exasperated by numerous political and cultural factors. Environmental science, for example, has been scorned by a good number of conservative US evangelicals because of its political ramifications. Discussion of ecological stewardship or "taking care of the earth" is considered by some to be "secular" and "liberal." Biblical scholar Sandra Richter demonstrates this very point in her telling of a time in which she and a fellow Wheaton College professor won a grant to launch the first-ever Wheaton College course designed specifically to integrate the Bible and biology:

We opened the first class with a seemingly innocent "ice-breaker": "Introduce yourself to the class, telling us your name, your major, and why you took this course." Like most teachers, I have deployed a conversation starter like this dozens of times in an array of classroom settings. But by the time this one was over, I was stunned. Why? Because *every* one of our twenty-some students voiced the same testimony: "I've always loved the outdoors (camping/hiking/bird watching/wild ponies on Assateague/the common dolphins in the Channel Island sound/the beauty of the Ozarks). I have always felt God's presence and pleasure when I pursued those loves. But as a Christian, I didn't think I was allowed to incorporate that love or advocacy for those loves into my Christian identity. So, I was really excited when you offered this course." *Every* student. Every well-educated, socially active, theologically committed young adult sitting in that classroom felt they were not allowed to advocate for the beauty and sanctity of God's creation and still call themselves "Christian."

We must ask: why is this such a common experience among evangelical Christians in the US?

As Richter points out, American politics is a definite factor. In the United States, if one is an environmentalist, it is assumed they are a Democrat. If one is a Republican, then, it is assumed that they cannot be pro-environment. And since many white evangelical Christians in the US vote Republican, because Democrats are not considered pro-life, environmental advocacy has been pigeonholed into a specific political profile and has in Richter's words, "become guilty by association." British biblical scholar and historian N. T. Wright has also made this point regarding the present American context.

> These issues [are] much harder for Americans to deal with than they are for the rest of us [in the world] . . . These are not major cultural issues for us. They do not carry—as I fear they often do in America—worryingly direct political implications. Clearly, the American issues are important. But it may help to reflect on how they are

bundled up with larger issues, gaining a lot of their apparent heat from those larger problems rather than from their own innate difficulties.

For those of us in the American context, we must consider how larger cultural issues may be distorting the way we view the relationship between Christian theology and the sciences.

Still, there are other reasons besides cultural/political ones that contribute to how Christians view the correlation between science and faith, which is that of biblical interpretation.

As a result of certain interpretations of Scripture, some Christians are left feeling as if they must choose between the Christian faith and scientific explanation. Irish Anglican theologian Alister McGrath, who serves as the professor of science and religion at the University of Oxford, has noted that because some evangelical Christians believe that the creation narratives in Genesis must be read as scientific texts, "the authority and clarity of Scripture—themes that are rightly cherished by evangelicals—seem to be at stake." Scriptural interpretation, then, is what leads some to assert that affirmation of anything outside a literal six-day creation and young earth, for example, is "anti-biblical."

Similarly, we see how various "rapture theologies" have also led some to believe that environmental stewardship is a waste of time. Christians who believe Scripture teaches that the present world is a bad thing, and the goal of the Christian life is to escape this material world, quite naturally assume that taking care of God's creation is pointless. As N. T. Wright puts it, "Why wallpaper the house if it's going to be knocked down tomorrow?" How we interpret Scripture, therefore, directly affects the way we think about the sciences.

So, the question we must ask ourselves is this: Are we reading Scripture correctly?

*

When we seek to approach the subject of science and theology, we must assert that Scripture is of supreme importance. However, an important assumption that must be named outright is that Scripture is of little use if we read it wrongly. I have become convinced that many well-meaning Christians have unknowingly confused Scripture with their interpretations of it. Put another way, sometimes in an attempt to defend Scripture, Christians have instead defended a specific *interpretation* of Scripture, rather than defending Scripture itself. If the presence of thousands upon thousands of Protestant denominations tells us anything, it is that the Bible can be read and interpreted in *many* ways. This is not to say that all readings of Scripture are equally valid. In fact, I am making the opposite claim: not all readings of Scripture ought to be considered equally acceptable.

Because we are finite creatures, we can easily misunderstand God's word. This is further complicated when we recognize that whether we like it or not, some passages of Scripture are more difficult to interpret than others, considering the issues of culture, language, and genre. As the apostle Paul reminds us, we currently see "through a glass, darkly" and know "only in part" (1 Cor 13:12, KJV). As McGrath further notes,

> Theology is not going to give you a clear-cut, unambiguous account of everything. The landscape of faith is not a sunlit-up land in which everything is clear and distinct; it remains partly obscured by mist and shadow. There are parallels here with the biblical descriptions of Moses approaching God, who is shrouded in cloud and darkness. We are wrestling with the living God, who overwhelms our capacity to understand and depict. Theologians use the term mystery to speak about God and salvation—not because our faith is irrational but because our limited capacities mean we cannot hope to grasp this in all its fullness.

When reading difficult, and dare I say, "controversial" texts such as Genesis 1, it benefits us when we come to the text with a spirit of humility. It also benefits us when we consult sage Christian interpreters who have read these texts before the dawn of modern science.

Centuries before Charles Darwin published *On the Origin of Species* (1859), Christian theologians interpreted the creation texts in a variety of ways. One of the most significant theologians of church history, Augustine (354–430), claimed in his final commentary on Genesis that the creation narrative referred to a historical event that must be understood in figurative and spiritual terms. Rather than the six days of creation being understood as literal twenty-four-hour days, he suggested that they are better understood as literary devices. Writing in the fourth century, Augustine put forward the idea that God created everything at once and that the seeds of creation generated life over time. An earlier theologian, Origen (185–253), believed something very similar: "Who would think that the first, second and third days of creation, which include an evening and a morning, could have existed without sun, moon, and stars? Who would think that the first day was without a sky? . . . No one doubts that these things are figures that speak of certain mysteries, the history having occurred symbolically and not literally." Basil of Caesarea (330–379) argued that the pattern of days serves to establish the world's relationship to eternity.

In my estimation, when it comes to interpreting Genesis 1, many well-meaning Christians unknowingly force a contemporary scientific reading upon an ancient, prescientific text. As Pentecostal theologian and minister Daniel Tomberlin explains:

> The creation narrative of Genesis 1 was not meant to be read from a modern historical or scientific perspective. Genesis 1 is theology . . . It proclaims there is one God who is Creator of all things. How does this ancient theological narrative apply to our scientific world? Science may help discover the *how* of creation. The inspired Scriptures proclaim the *Who* of creation.

Reading Genesis rightly and responsibly means we seek to read it as it was intended to be read.

When Copernicus proved that the sun rather than the earth was at the center of the universe, theologians challenged his work based on particular interpretations of the Bible (Josh 10:12–13, for instance). However, we have since realized that there are more faithful ways of reading such texts. What we can discover then, in Tomberlin's words, is that often "the conflict between science and faith is not in what the Bible says, but how we choose to interpret the Bible." Speaker and writer on science and faith issues Greg Cootsona has stated, "When Psalm 8 and Psalm 19 lead us to consider the heavens and the glory of humankind, they don't tell us how to use a telescope, interpret the mathematics of physics, or understand comparative anatomy." Rather the psalms are urging believers to consider the majesty of God and his creative handiwork. As Galileo once quipped, the Holy Spirit intends to teach us how one goes to heaven, not how heaven goes. Therefore, I am convinced that Genesis 1 is best read theologically rather than scientifically. Why? Because that, I believe, is the way it was always intended to be read. From this significant chapter of Scripture, we discover that God created *all* life on earth and created humanity uniquely in God's image. And those facts cannot be gleaned from science.

*

In the seventeenth century, it was a common belief that God had written two books: the book of Scripture and the book of nature. Both were to be read, and if this was done properly there could be no inconsistency or disagreement between them since they both were written by the same Author. However, this perspective changed in the eighteenth century. When Isaac Newton's heirs became enchanted by the deterministic character of his equations, it was thought that we lived in a closed, mechanical world implying that "God" was now irrelevant to the discussion. Since then, some have continued to hold this view even despite advancements in science that might suggest otherwise. Still, the common, "on-the-ground" assumption among many today is the same: science and faith cannot be reconciled.

However, I believe the basic insight of the seventeenth-century scientific "fathers" is worth a reexamination. Even if persons such as Galileo and Newton had problems with Christian orthodoxy, their essential observation that modern science and religious belief ought not to compete is an important suggestion. This proposal has gained much support in the last few decades as Christian theologians and scientists have begun more intentional dialogues. One of the major voices in this conversation has been John Polkinghorne, the former professor of mathematical physics at Cambridge University and Anglican priest. As he sees it, "If science and theology are both concerned with the search for truth, they are friends and not foes." Because God is both creator and revealer, Christians should contend for the mutual interaction between science and theology. In Polkinghorne's view:

> Science is concerned with the question, How?—By what process do things happen? Theology is concerned with the question, Why?—Is there a meaning and purpose behind what is happening? We are perfectly familiar with the fact that we can ask and answer both questions about the same event. The kettle is boiling because burning gas heats the water. The kettle is burning because I want to make a cup of tea . . . We do not need to choose between these two answers, and, in fact, if we are fully to understand the event of the boiling kettle, we need them both.

Pope John Paul II fosters this idea when he notes that while "science can purify religion from error and superstition; religion can purify science from idolatry and false absolutes. Each can draw the other into a wider world, a world in which both can flourish." This is exactly right—science and theology ought to cooperate, recognizing that both can reveal truth. Though this is a good reminder for Christian theologians, pastors, and ordinary lay Christians, it is also a good reminder for those within the scientific community. As biologist F. J. J. Buytendijk once noted, "To put it simply: birds sing more than they ought to do according to Darwin." From a Christian perspective, scientific and theological reflection on creation can be acts of worship to our Creator.

*

Christians believe that God has made his creation "very good" (Gen 1:31). In this way, our children's prayer is exactly right: The world is "sweet." Creation testifies to God's beauty and majesty: "The heavens are telling the glory of God, and the firmament proclaims his handiwork" (Ps 19:1). But because the earth belongs to God and not us (Ps 24:1), having "dominion" over it (Gen 1:26) means exercising responsible study, care, and stewardship, helping all of creation to flourish in life and for life as intended. In the words of Daniel Migliore, "it is a 'dominion' of care and protection rather than of domination and abuse." We must recognize how this illuminates our prayer: Because God is the one who has provided "the food we eat," "the bird that sings" and "everything," we must thank God not only with our mouths but with our hands. We have been commissioned to be good stewards of what God has created. Taking care of the created order thus can be understood as an act of worship to God.

As Gus Speth, former administrator of the United Nations Sustainable Development Group, once stated,

> I used to think that the top environmental problems were biodiversity loss, ecosystem collapse, and climate change. I thought that thirty years of good science could address these problems. I was wrong. The top environmental problems are selfishness, greed, and apathy, and to deal with these we need a cultural and spiritual transformation. And we scientists don't know how to do that.

Speth rightly notes that addressing environmental issues requires deep cultural and spiritual renewal. In light of this, Christians ought to be motivated to action. Ecological activities are central to our faith not because we are motivated by secular agendas, but because we are called to care for and steward what God has created.

When we are obedient to fulfilling God's call, not only can God's creation further flourish, but we too can further thrive in our discipleship. Though the world is not as it will be because of the fall (Gen 3), all things were created in, through, and for Christ (Col 1:16–17). One day, all of creation will be resurrected and restored (Rom 8:22–23) along with our bodies (1 Cor 15). Then, the wolf will dwell in peace with the lamb and children will play with scorpions (Isa 11). But until that time, we are commissioned to be stewards of creation, worshiping and thanking our God who has created this "sweet" world.

According to Richter, joining a responsible environmental organization, buying organic and recycled as much as possible, living with restraint, learning how and where to recycle responsibly, helping your church, school, and office begin recycling, addressing your consumption of energy, attending to your automobile, giving up chemical lawn service, and joining a community-supported agriculture group are all examples of how Christians might practically live out their commitment and care for the created order. When we practice creation care, there are positive implications for both creation and us.

*

Far from threatening my faith, gleaning from scientific discovery has given me a deeper appreciation and awe for our Creator. Contemplating creation fills me with wonder and gratitude. Theologians and scientists both investigate God's world, which we have been given to study and appreciate. Turning from infancy to adulthood in this regard means moving beyond cultural wars. It means adopting a grander perspective of God's activity in the world and learning to read the book of Scripture and the book of nature more meekly and maturely. And it means living sensibly before God as we love and cherish where he has placed us. When we can adopt such a perspective, we can move beyond living out of fear and intimidation, and into joy and delight.

For Reflection or Discussion

As you pray this children's prayer in light of this chapter, consider reflecting on and/or discussing the following questions:

1. Do you tend to see science and faith as "friends or foes"? Why?

2. "Sometimes in an attempt to defend Scripture, Christians have instead defended a specific *interpretation* of Scripture, rather than defending Scripture itself." Think of a belief or understanding you once had regarding Scripture that has shifted or changed as you have grown. What does that say to you about approaching the interpretation of Scripture with humility?

3. When thinking of science and the Bible, particularly the creation narrative, God-loving, orthodox believers interpret these passages differently. Thus, is it appropriate to make the interpretation of these texts the litmus test for authentic faith? Why or why not?

4. John Polkinghorne states, "Science is concerned with the question, How?—By what process do things happen? Theology is concerned with the question, Why?—Is there a meaning and purpose behind what is happening?" Does this resonate with you? Why or why not?

5. Has your faith tradition endorsed care and stewardship of creation or a view that "taking care of God's creation is pointless"? Which approach more aligns with Scripture and the Christian tradition?

4

Protected by God

Lord, keep us safe this night,
Secure from all our fears;
May angels guard us while we sleep,
Till morning light appears.

SOME children experience night terrors. I first experienced mine as a young adolescent. I would periodically wake up in overwhelming horror. As a result, I could not fall back to sleep, no matter how much I tried. During those years, the only way I was able to fall back asleep was by listening to nineties Christian worship music on my parents' Walkman. After a few songs, I would begin to experience calm and slip back into sleep.

Though we expect ourselves to move on from evening fear, most adults still prefer the light of day to the darkness of nightfall. And this is not merely for pragmatic reasons. Let's face it—darkness can be eerie. Perhaps this is one reason, among others, why darkness develops into such a rich source of metaphor for spiritual realities. In Scripture, darkness is ignorance (Ps 82:5), falsehood (1 John 1:16), and folly (Prov 2:13). It is the human mind without God's revelation (2 Pet 1:19). Since light represents goodness, evildoers are those who rebel against the light (Job 24:13). According to Jesus, those who love evil "hate the light" (John 3:20). And Paul instructs the early believers in Rome to "lay aside the works of darkness and put on the armor of light" (Rom 13:12).

Our children's prayer centers around light and darkness both literally and metaphorically. As any good evening prayer does, it petitions God to keep one safe at night, protected from fears, guarded by heavenly beings, until the light of morn appears. But do we ever outgrow such prayers? Some of us might think so. However, I am not convinced.

*

If fear is a disease, everyone has been infected. Though we all want to hope, too often we find ourselves entangled in fear and anxiety. The idea of progress based on science, technology, and education has not helped us move into hopefulness as many suggested it would. We still grapple with fear. Progress in knowledge has not been paralleled with progress in morality. Science, technology, and education have brought about many benefits, but they are also the factors that have brought about Hiroshima.

Much has been made over the fact that we now live in an "atomic age." Surely, at least for those who think about it, this can prove to be a bit unsettling. However, fear of the unexpected and catastrophic is not something we face today alone. In C. S. Lewis's opinion,

> In one way we think a great deal too much of the atomic bomb. "How are we to live in an atomic age?" I am tempted to reply: "Why, as you would have lived in the sixteenth century when the plague visited London almost every year, or as you would have lived in a Viking age when raiders from Scandinavia might land and cut your throat any night; or indeed, as you are already living in an age of cancer, an age of syphilis, an age of paralysis, an age of air raids, an age of railway accidents, an age of motor accidents.

Fear accompanies people in every age of human history. Make no mistake, we are all afraid of something.

But perhaps humanity's most consistent fear is the dread of *ultimate* darkness—the grave. Here in the US, we have built billion-dollar industries to support us in both delaying and ignoring death. Medicine, however good it is in postponing death, cannot save us from it. Entertainment, too, may help us forget about our mortality, but we will eventually face it. All will eventually experience "the place of no return . . . utter darkness" (Job 10:21–22).

In an in-depth interview with *The New York Times*, American television and radio show host Larry King revealed that he is a believer in cryonics, the low-temperature freezing and storage of a human corpse or severed head. Along with others, King prepared to have his body frozen and then thawed out when researchers discover a cure for whatever killed him. Though King stated that he would not be surprised if those behind cryonics are "nuts," he considered it worth a shot, giving him a chance to die with at least "some hope." Along with King, we cannot avoid thinking about the future. All of us must reckon with it. In fact, whether we live in fear or hope depends a great deal on what we perceive to be in our own future.

But this is where we can lean in to our children's prayer: we can trust in the Lord to keep us safe as we experience night—he can overcome our fears. We rest at night *in hope*. Martin Luther has a good translation of John 16:33: "In the world you have anxiety. But be confident, I have overcome the world." Hope, then, is essentially confidence in our future—not needing to fear—because we faithfully trust in what God has done in Christ through the Spirit. God, who is the source of hope, may fill us with joy and peace as we trust in him (Rom 15:13). In Catholic theologian Karl Rahner's words, we can experience hope since Christ enacted "the irreversible beginning of the coming of God as the absolute future of the universe." As Jesus says, "Because I live, you also will live" (John 14:19). In Christ, we can face the dark.

*

If this children's prayer is about anything, it is about finding safety and rest in God. However, part of the way we experience this safety and rest is through angelic protection. What might we make of our prayer's reference to angels?

The poem "The Angel" by English poet William Blake is helpful here:

> I dreamt a dream! What can it mean?
> And that I was a maiden Queen
> Guarded by an Angel mild:
> Witless woe was ne'er beguiled!
>
> And I wept both night and day,
> And he wiped my tears away;
> And I wept both day and night,
> And hid from him my heart's delight.
>
> So he took his wings, and fled;
> Then the morn blushed rosy red.
> I dried my tears, and armed my fears
> With ten thousand shields and spears.
>
> Soon my Angel came again;
> I was armed, he came in vain;
> For the time of youth was fled,
> And grey hairs were on my head.

No doubt this poem lends itself to a multiplicity of readings. However, as I read it, I find myself reflecting on the ways in which we have been trained to "outgrow" innocently trusting celestial beings, including God. As with the young queen, it is easy to find comfort in God and guardian angels when we are young. However, we are eventually stripped of our early innocence. Any suggestion of believing in angelic beings at this later point in our lives is "in vain." The narration of an innocent, youthful queen becoming a skeptical, grey-haired warrior is illustrative of our own lives. And this is not isolated to only ordinary Christians. Christian theologians and pastors struggle too. I know.

The father of modern liberal theology, Friedrich Schleiermacher, epitomized the cynicism of the last few centuries when he raised the question of whether there is any real need for angels in

Christian theology. Certainly, there are those today that are sympathetic to such a suggestion. According to most religious scholars in the twentieth century, the notion of angels, fallen or unfallen, is hardly believable. And yet, the "ecumenical-orthodox" theologian Donald Bloesch has humorously noted that "the demise of belief in angels has been accompanied by the rise of belief in flying saucers and extraterrestrial beings from outer space."

Even though quite a few religious scholars would still balk at the reality of spirits today, there is a resurgence of interest and belief in angels and spiritual experiences in the general population. Yes, non-theistic naturalism has gripped the minds and hearts of countless people in the West, but in no way is this wholesale. Many today find themselves able to reject the false dichotomy of *either* God *or* scientific explanation. It is indeed possible to take seriously the scientific accounts of reality while also being open to a spirit-filled universe. The petition "may angels guard us while we sleep," then, may not be as absurd as some might imagine.

Surely the biblical authors were not bothered by the notion of angels interceding and ministering to people. In Scripture, angels are messengers (Matt 4:6). They can appear like humans and converse with people (Gen 18:1–8; Luke 1:11–38). They are guardians and protectors of the people of God (Ps 34:7; Ps 91:11–12). It is this final feature of angels that our prayer holds up—God protects his people through angels as servants of God.

When it comes to believing in angels or believing in anything for that matter, neither blind innocence nor critical cynicism is the answer. Instead, we are to construct a vision of the world that makes sense of what has been revealed to us. For Christians, this means that we look at the revelation of Jesus and how that disclosure relates to everything else around us. This is what it means to do theology. Monk, theologian, and archbishop Anselm of Canterbury (1033–1109), defined theology as "faith seeking understanding." This suggests that the Christian faith puts in motion a mission to know and understand God and how all things relate to God. However, we cannot equate "understanding" with mastery. Reason at its highest leads us to the edge of mystery. As Paul says to the church in Corinth, "we speak the wisdom of God in a mystery" (1 Cor 2:7, KJV). When it comes to the reality of angels, Protestant scholar Claus Westermann has proposed that whether we like it or not, "angels are as inaccessible as God himself."

Australian theologian Steve Wright, I believe, is exactly right in his suggestion that we can only speak of angels as we speak of any mystery: "as pure poetry." Perhaps most famously, the Italian poet, writer, and philosopher Dante spent much time writing poetry about angels. And though there was much he was mistaken about regarding the afterlife, his descriptions of angels are right insofar as they leave us in wonderment. Angels ought to have that kind of effect on us. I do believe that angels should not be reduced to mere metaphors. In other words, we are completely justified in believing in the reality of angelic agents. However, that belief ought not to propel us towards an overly speculative rationalization of them. Our children's prayer is right in keeping God at the center of our references to angels. Talk of angels, at best, moves us towards awe of God's goodness and provision for us.

*

Just as darkness is a metaphor for evil and the evil one, so is light a metaphor for goodness and the Good One. The final picture of light that we find in Scripture appears in the book of Revelation. Here the new Jerusalem descends from heaven and contains the "glory of God and a radiance like a very rare jewel, like jasper, clear as crystal" (Rev 21:11). The city has no need for "light of lamp or sun, for the Lord God will be their light, and they will reign forever and ever" (Rev 22:5). Here light symbolizes our glorious future in God where the darkness of death "will be no more" (Rev 21:4). Thus, when we pray for God's safety "till morning light appears," we are petitioning God to sustain us providentially until we reach God's glorious End.

But how might we best speak of God's providential oversight?

Because the world is created and sustained by God, God holds all things together. This means that everything that happens is at the very least *permitted* by God. However, it is also true there is much that goes on in this world that is *not* God's will and grieves the heart of God. Rather than seeking a tidy and oversimplified explanation of how all this works out, I think it is best to admit, in Scottish theologian David Fergusson's words, that "there is a surd element in life that remains incomprehensible." But even amid the incomprehensibility, we can hope in God's providential workings both now and in the future. We can hope in his care for us today and tomorrow. We can consider Jesus' promise to his disciples: "Remember, I am with you always, to the end of the age" (Matt 28:20). Or to put it another way, he is with us as we await "the morning" to once again "appear."

Until the "morning light appears," we rest in God's wisdom and care. No matter the darkness around us, we can celebrate God's decisive victory. This "till"—the time between our salvation and ultimate redemption—is not a call towards complacent waiting, then, but rather active anticipation. As the church, we operate in futuristic newness. Through the church's worship and mission, we seek to proclaim the things *to come* even amid the things *that are*.

But we are not often used to talking about the End in these ways. In my own American religious context, I often find that by and large Christians have been misled in their thinking and living as it relates to the End. Fundamentalist sermons and books proclaiming the imminent end of the world continue to be written, delivered, and sold. Even when said events do not come to pass, these self-proclaimed prophets and teachers continue to get a wide hearing. This kind of "neo-apocalypticism" feeds on fear. Certainly, many are familiar with these visions of the End. Reformed theologian Daniel Migliore describes it perfectly:

> Neo-apocalypticism . . . offers to allay this fear by describing the exact timetable of the awful events of the end as ordained by God and predicted by the Bible. With the reestablishment of the modern state of Israel as a base date, and drawing on a few obscure texts in Ezekiel, Daniel, 1 Thessalonians, and the book of Revelation, neo-apocalypticism identifies the biblical battle of Armageddon with a coming thermonuclear holocaust. True believers will be "raptured" or caught up in the clouds to

be with the Lord (1 Thess 4:17). Rescued by Christ out of a world plunging toward destruction, they will not have to endure the terrible years of tribulation. The return of Jesus Christ and the rapture of faithful Christians from the terrible end times is, according to [Hal] Lindsey, "the real hope for the Christian, the blessed hope of true believers." By God's plan, the responsibility for evangelizing the earth during those years will be assigned to 144,000 converted Jews. All this will happen, readers are warned, in their lifetime.

It is hard to overstate how popular these teachings are in American evangelicalism. It is also hard to overstate how wrong this vision of the End truly is.

According to the New Testament, Christian hope is not centered on a rapture. Neither the word "rapture" nor the idea of a rapture is present within the New Testament itself. Instead, the Christian hope rests on the redemptive power of God, whose judgment is real, but whose mercy endures forever. The End is not only ahead of us but among us. In Jesus' words, "the kingdom of God has come near" (Mark 1:15). Wesleyan American theologian Beth Felker Jones rightly notes that

> we must realize that Christian teaching regarding the "last things" not only impacts the future but also the present. Last things such as heaven, hell, death, judgment, the second coming of Christ, and the kingdom of God are already becoming present realities because of what Christ has set into motion through his death and resurrection.

This point is furthered when we consider what it means to say that Jesus is "coming soon" (Rev 22:12). In *The Voyage of the Dawn Treader*, Aslan looks at Lucy and tells her, "Do not be sad Lucy. We will see each other soon." Lucy replies, "Please Aslan, what do you mean by 'soon'?" Fittingly, Aslan replies, "I call all time soon." Thinking about Christ's coming in this way can help us understand what theologians call the "already but not yet" of Christ's kingdom. He has come and he is coming. Because of this, all time is soon.

As I suggested earlier, this way of thinking about the End helps us live differently. Rather than standing around, we ought to pay attention to the question spoken to those who had just witnessed Christ's ascension: "Men of Galilee, why do you stand looking up toward heaven? This Jesus, who has been taken up from you into heaven, will come in the same way as you saw him go into heaven" (Acts 1:11). Living in Christ's "soon" means living a life of service and mission to Christ's body and the world. Felker-Jones, again, is helpful here:

> We are to live in the expectation of Christmas Eve, our sleep unsettled by the excitement of what is coming. Ours is the joyous expectation of a nesting mother preparing for the birth of a new baby, busy and active in preparation for what is to come. Ours is also the expectation of a people whose hope gives us power, allowing us to speak truth in a world of lies and to embody love in a world of hate.

*

While I have not experienced night terrors since I was young, as an adult I have faced several seasons filled with dark nights. At times, anxiety and depression have gripped me. I have experienced what St. John of the Cross called "the dark night of the soul." Still, I have never been without true hope. Even as I walked in the darkest valley, God was with me (Ps 23:4). I was "guarded" and kept "safe." I can assuredly echo the psalmist in declaring that even "if I make my bed in the depths, you are there" (Ps 139:8).

Therefore, moving from infancy to maturity does not mean we move on *from* dependence, but rather *toward* it. Maturity in Christ is marked by a true recognition of how dependent we truly are. Only then can we begin to "taste and see that the Lord is good," despite the difficulty (Ps 34:8). Only then can we sense the presence of God with us until the very end of the age (Matt 28:18). And only then can we begin to live into the mission and service that God has for us "till morning light appears."

For Reflection or Discussion

As you pray this children's prayer in light of this chapter, consider reflecting on and/or discussing the following questions:

1. What are the areas or issues that cause you the greatest fear? How would you face these fears differently if you believed—truly believed—that you are completely secure in God's hands?

2. If hope dispels fear, as light dispels darkness, think of/share a time when, as an adult, you were afraid until "light" broke through, and you were able to see things as they really were rather than through the lens of your fear.

3. Revisit the following statement from Beth Felker-Jones: "Ours is also the expectation of a people whose hope gives us power, allowing us to speak truth in a world of lies and to embody love in a world of hate." How does hope for the future consummation of all things embolden you to live out these words in your context?

4. Do you have greater difficulty trusting in God's protection for "eternal" things or "temporal" things? Why do you think that is the case?

5

Delivered by God

*From ghoulies and ghosties
and longleggitie beasties
and things that go bump in the night,
Good Lord, deliver us.*

Both of my daughters have gone through phases when they feared "monsters" under their beds or in their closets. Of course, when they expressed their concern, my wife and I always assured them to the contrary. Still, they often felt unsure.

But recently my youngest's fear seemed to be once and for all pacified after watching the 2001 animated film *Monsters, Inc.* If you have seen the film, you know that it is set in Monstropolis—a city populated completely by monsters and powered by energy from the screams of human children. Because of the city's energy needs, experienced monsters are hired as "scarers" who venture into the human world to frighten children and collect their screams. However, things go awry when a two-year-old girl follows one of the scarers, Sulley, back into the monster world. As one might expect, this creates much trouble for Sulley and his friend Mike. However, Sulley eventually bonds with the girl and becomes aware of how traumatizing his scaring can be for human children. In the end,

Sulley changes the scaring policy when he becomes CEO of the company. Monsters are then tasked with collecting human children's laughs instead of their screams.

For children, the movie provides entertainment and laughs, but also comfort. By being introduced to monsters such as Mike Wazowski (Billy Crystal) and James P. "Sulley" Sullivan (John Goodman), children, such as my daughter, are offered an alternative imaginary world where monsters are loving and lovable, rather than diabolic and sinister. Consequently, it has become clear to me that the way children perceive "monsters" can deeply influence their experiences of the world. And the same is true for adults. Like children, what we believe about "ghoulies," "ghosties," or "longleggitie beasties" impacts the way we view God, the world, and ultimately, our lives.

*

While most people will affirm that true evil exists in the world, a more debated topic in our modern society is whether something like supernatural evil exists. Ever since the dawn of the Enlightenment or the "age of reason" in the seventeenth and eighteenth centuries, Western societies have questioned the reality of spirits. As such, angels and demons became an embarrassment to those Christian theologians who desired to convey the faith in an age of science and rationalism. As the notable Baptist theologian Bernard Ramm appropriately articulated, spirits "seem to intrude upon science like the unexpected visit of the country relatives to their rich city kinsfolk." Even among contemporary people who continue to believe in the "Great Spirit" (God), belief in lesser spirits, such as angels and demons, is waning.

But Kärkkäinen is right in calling this trend into question. In his words, "How can one believe in the 'Great(est) Spirit,' God, and fail to be open to the workings of 'smaller spirits' created by the same God?" In his view, the refusal to recognize other spirits has to do with the rise of naturalism rather than the rise of science itself. Because naturalism is a philosophical view that asserts all there is, is nature, it is *an ideological* view of the world. This means that scientific explanations do not undermine Christian theology. To make this claim, we should not try to harmonize theology with science or attempt to harmonize science with theology. Instead, we ought to contend for *mutual* interaction between theology and science. Considered from a Christian perspective, both reflect on the world God has made, so they ought to have reciprocal engagement. Again, in Kärkkäinen's words, this means theology does not merely "serve as science's religious interpreter but should also challenge and contribute to science's quest." Similarly, British physicist-priest John Polkinghorne has noted that "if science and theology are both concerned with the search for truth, they are friends and not foes." One way theology can contribute to the dialogue, then, is to remind such communities that scientific explanations of the world do not inevitably negate a spirit-filled universe.

This realization paired with insights gleaned from non-Western societies can help us realize that we ought not to "rationalize away" the presence of spirits in the world. We have good reason, then, to resist reducing spirits to mere metaphor. However, we must also resist developing overly conjectural accounts of them. C. S. Lewis famously observed that Christians often fall into one of two errors relating to the devil and evil spirits: They either believe such agents do not exist, or they give them much more attention and power than they merit.

An example of the latter error can be found in the Middle Ages. Christians at the time often fixated on angels and demons, developing highly speculative descriptions. Supposedly, some medieval theologians even speculated as to how many angels can stand on a point of a needle. This seemingly nonsensical question was posed to provoke conversation around spiritual creatures and spatial dimensions. Still, are such speculative questions warranted? In his poem, "Questions about Angels," contemporary American poet Billy Collins humorously responds:

> Of all the questions you might want to ask
> about angels, the only one you ever hear
> is how many can dance on the head of a pin.

Delivered by God

No curiosity about how they pass the eternal time
besides circling the Throne chanting in Latin
or delivering a crust of bread to a hermit on earth
or guiding a boy and girl across a rickety wooden bridge.

Do they fly through God's body and come out singing?
Do they swing like children from the hinges
of the spirit world saying their names backwards and forwards?
Do they sit alone in little gardens changing colors?

What about their sleeping habits, the fabric of their robes,
their diet of unfiltered divine light?
What goes on inside their luminous heads? Is there a wall
these tall presences can look over and see hell?

If an angel fell off a cloud, would he leave a hole
in a river and would the hole float along endlessly
filled with the silent letters of every angelic word?

If an angel delivered the mail, would he arrive
in a blinding rush of wings or would he just assume
the appearance of the regular mailman and
whistle up the driveway reading the postcards?

No, the medieval theologians control the court.
The only question you ever hear is about
the little dance floor on the head of a pin
where halos are meant to converge and drift invisibly.

It is designed to make us think in millions,
billions, to make us run out of numbers and collapse
into infinity, but perhaps the answer is simply one:
one female angel dancing alone in her stocking feet,
a small jazz combo working in the background.

She sways like a branch in the wind, her beautiful
eyes closed, and the tall thin bassist leans over
to glance at his watch because she has been dancing
forever, and now it is very late, even for musicians.

What seems to be clear is that Collins's poem is a commentary on not merely his opinions on religion and angels, but the way the church has sought to curate and control such questions and answers. The first stanza includes the line: "the only one you ever hear is how many angels can dance on the head of a pin." This line, paired with the speaker's remark that "medieval theologians control the court," seems to signal that the speaker believes that the church is asking the wrong kinds of questions, and in doing so is killing individual "curiosity" about other important matters. Using irony, Collins shows that the answers we most desire might be simpler than the church often makes them.

Such critiques ought to give us pause. Though we might want to push back on several fronts, Christian theologians and church leaders would do well to sit introspectively with Collins's critiques. At the very least, this poem ought to jolt us into asking ourselves whether our discussions around spiritual agents reveal us to be overly fascinated with them. Medieval Christians are not the only ones guilty of moving into excessive captivation with angels and demons. My own tribe, Pentecostal/Charismatic Christians, for instance, are often guilty of this. While Christians ought to be commended for taking spiritual realities seriously, we should also take great caution to *not* move beyond what has been revealed to us. In fact, it would be wise to remember that Christian Scripture is strongly opposed to any form of superstition.

Considering these common mistakes—either denying the reality of spiritual agents altogether or giving them more attention than they merit—it becomes clear that there is an ongoing need for reconstructed reflections on spiritual realities. So, we must ask: what are these spiritual agents? And how are we to comprehend the nature and place of spiritual realities within the world God has made?

*

According to Christian thought, the world is not as it should be or better yet, *as it will be*. We are told that in the beginning, God created things "good" (Gen 1), but through sin, things have gone amiss (Gen 3). Because "good" does not mean "perfect," immature humanity was able to choose disobedience. As Irenaeus has argued, the mystery of finite liberty and God's permissive will is what allowed evil to shape the world. As a result, not only is humanity caught up in evil, but angelic agents are as well.

According to the New Testament, not only are there "good" angels but there are also others who have "left their proper dwelling" (Jude 6; 2 Peter 2:4). Like angels, demons are spiritual agents, but unlike angels who serve as God's ministers, demons serve Satan or the devil. Overall, demons work to frustrate God's work and torment humanity (Matt 12:22–32; Mark 3:3:22–30; Luke 11:14–23).

We also discover that Satan is the chief of demons. According to Jesus, Satan is the ruler of this world (John 12:31; 14:30; 16:11). Similarly, Paul describes him as the "god of this world" (2 Cor 4:4) and as the "ruler of the power of the air" (Eph 2:2). Further, according to African theologian J. Nkansah-Obrempong,

> Satan is the agent who tempts Jesus in the wilderness after his baptism (Matt 4:1–11), and he is cast into the lake of fire after the last conflict between God and the Devil (Rev 20:10). The Bible calls him by other names. He is called the serpent (Gen 3:1–7; Rev 12:9, 14–15; 20:2), Lucifer (Is 14:12–15), destroyer (Rev 9:11), and described as a Dragon (Rev 12:1–17; 20:2). His other names include murderer (John 8:44), deceiver (Rev 12:9), tempter (Matt 4:3), adversary (1 Peter 5:8), father of lies (John 8:44), and many others.

This much is clear from Scripture: Satan and the demonic are agents that exert power on the world. Nonetheless, this power ought to be put into proper perspective. Satan is *not* a "rival god" in any sense. In Christian thought, there is only one God! What Scripture reveals instead is that Satan and his followers do exert true influence in this world, but that they cannot supersede limits placed upon them. Though Satan is a powerful being, he is not all-powerful. The gospel promises that God, the all-great and all-good one, will defeat the evil in the world that has been caused by Satan and his evil forces.

*

Though we ought to affirm that evil spiritual agents are indeed personal, our children's prayer also seems to talk about nonpersonal evil. While there are evil personal agents—"ghoulies, ghosties, and longleggitie beasties"—there is also nonpersonal evil—"*things* that go bump in the night." Though our discussion must begin with personal evil, it must also include discussion of nonpersonal evil. Thus, we must also speak about the more corporate relationship between the world of spirits and human existence. In other words, we must also talk about societal structures that are demonic in character. The evangelical theologian Stanley Grenz is quite helpful on this front.

According to Grenz, all human life is inevitably bound with structures of existence. For instance, religious, intellectual, moral, and political structures are established and formed by human social interaction. Though created and utilized by human beings, in some sense the structures lie outside of human control. Economic, political, and moral societal norms are influenced not only by humans, then, but also by what the apostle Paul calls "the powers." From a biblical perspective, while these structures were created good (Col 1:16), they now stand in opposition to God and Christ, and therefore, to us (Col 2:8). Those who obey them have become enslaved to them (Gal 4:8–11). We are then called to battle them (Eph 6:12), and we can do so considering that Christ has disarmed the powers on the cross (Col 2:14–15). Ultimately, Christ is the victor. He will defeat the world structure that remains evil, but as long as we live in a broken world, we face broken systems that have been infected by sin.

According to Canadian Baptist theologian Clark Pinnock,

> Sin affects the structures of the world, and we oppose sin in all its manifestations, including our own complicity in what is wrong. Conversion points, then, not only to individual change but beyond to the coming transformation

of the world. Since we are creatures in society and in a world, God wants to renew both us and our created context. If God did not intend that, he would be tackling half the problem. Social sanctification and cosmic renewal are ultimately part of God's plan.

Pinnock is right. Sin has affected both individuals and corporate structures, thus we should strive not only for individual sanctification but social sanctification. He is also correct in stating, though, that true change and transformation that lasts will only be possible with the coming of God. Therefore, we continue to pray, as children, "Good Lord, deliver us."

*

Early on in my Christian journey, I heard a lot about how Jesus' death put us right with God, but I never understood *how* it did so. I knew that Jesus' death was "for me" (Gal 2:20), "for us" (Rom 5:8), "for many" (Mark 10:45), and "for all" (2 Cor 5:14–15). But I still wondered—why did Christ have to die in order to accomplish redemption?

Fortunately, in seminary I discovered that Christians throughout the ages have thought deeply about this question. Perhaps the most familiar answer is what theologians call the "satisfaction" view. In short, this view states that Jesus had to live and die because humanity has dishonored God through disobedience. Since God is just, he cannot forgive sin without payment for the lost honor. So, satisfaction is needed. As such, Jesus paid the satisfaction through his perfect obedience and voluntary death on the cross. Satisfaction is then executed, justice made, God's honor reinstated, and sinners are absolved. Paul says something similar when he tells the Galatians that "Christ redeemed us from the curse of the law by becoming a curse for us" (Gal 3:13).

However, as helpful as this explanation is, it says little about God delivering us from Satan and the evil powers. Also, some versions of the "satisfaction" view can give the impression that the Father hates sinners and cannot love them until his wrath is appeased. Certainly this is not the case! It was his love for us that moved him to send his Son for us in the first place (Rom 5:8). The missing piece in many discussions around Jesus' death and our salvation has to do with Christ coming to save us from genuine evil. As our children's prayer notes, there is an important connection between spiritual agents and God's deliverance. As Paul puts it, through his death and resurrection, Jesus "disarmed the rulers and authorities and made a public example of them, triumphing over them in it" (Col 2:15). Therefore, how might we better account for this connection?

Though often overlooked in church circles today, for the first thousand years of Christian history, most Christians believed Jesus lived and died to not only provide "satisfaction" but to also enact victory over evil powers. Since humanity has been enslaved to such powers, Jesus came to redeem us and set us free. This explanation is often called the "*Christus victor*" or "Christ the victor" view.

Consider second-century bishop Irenaeus's explanation. In his view, by taking on flesh, Jesus has "summed up all things" in himself. According to Irenaeus, Jesus—the God-man—became victorious where the rest of humanity has failed and therefore is able to "undo" what we have done. The apostle Paul suggests something similar when he talks about Christ being the last Adam (1 Cor 15:45–49): Christ is the Last Adam who is victorious where the first Adam failed. Within this framework, Christ has come to take on our humanity to defeat Satan, sin, and death so that we can participate in God's life anew.

Related is early church bishop and theologian Gregory of Nyssa's view. According to Gregory, Jesus' death is like a fish unsuspectingly swallowing the bait on a fishhook. Under the veil of his humanity was Christ's divinity, and once Satan swallowed the bait, Christ triumphed over him, the demons, and all the powers that hold humanity captive. Humanity is set free due to Jesus' death and resurrection.

But why might this be important?

When we place all the emphasis upon the death of Christ and take no interest in the triumph of Christ over death, we miss out on the very goal of our redemption, which is union with God. In

Christ, God not only saved us *from* sin, but he saved us *for* union with Him. The *Christus victor* view can help us better comprehend how Jesus' death and resurrection can free us *from* the evil one and *for* God. As Lossky puts it, Christ's saving activity in his life, death, and resurrection "is seen to be directly related to the ultimate goal of creatures: to know union with God." Pardon or acquittal is just the beginning. Salvation is a process of having Christ formed in us (Gal 4:19) and becoming partakers of God's divine nature (2 Pet 1:4).

In Ephesians 5, Paul instructs husbands and wives to "submit to one another out of reverence for Christ" and further instructs husbands to "love [their] wives, just as Christ loved the church and gave himself up for her." Paul is clear that marriage is a sign and wonder of the mutual love that exists between Christ and his church. In other words, human marriage is a sign that points beyond itself: it points beyond human love *to* divine love. This is exactly why throughout Christian history, the biblical book Song of Songs has been read not only as a song celebrating human love but as a song that is symbolic of Christ's love for his bride, the church. Many Christians have heard in it a hymn of Christ's love for the church and a song about humanity's innate longing for the presence of God. The mystical writer Bernard of Clairvaux writing in the 1100s (1090–1153) penned eighty-six sermons on the Song of Songs and barely made it past the second chapter.

Therefore, when we hear the Song declare "your love is more delightful than wine" (Song 1:2), we might consider that a spiritual reading captures the beauty of the process of union with God over a lifetime. Anyone who knows anything about wine knows that the longer it ages, the better it tastes. So, as we progress in our union with God, we will quite naturally begin to be swept deeper into the beauty of God's love.

In sum, these reflections can help us comprehend that the goal of our deliverance is participation in God.

*

Like the apostle Paul, when I was a child, "I spoke like a child, I thought like a child, I reasoned like a child; but when I became an adult, I put an end to childish ways" (1 Cor 13:11). Part of putting an end to my childish ways was to begin thinking more seriously about spiritual agents and realities. As I become more mature in Christ, rather than being delivered from the difficulty of discernment, I found myself pushed deeper into it. But as a result, I was able to arrive at a more mature vision of the world. I was able to reject my later tendency to minimize the reality of spirits through rationalization and move beyond my early eccentric and superstitious fascination with them. In the end, I was better able to trust in God, rather than in my cognitive constructs or imaginative inventions. Finally, I am now able to pray "Good Lord, deliver us," with mature dependence.

For Reflection or Discussion

As you pray this children's prayer in light of this chapter, consider reflecting on and/or discussing the following questions:

1. What has been your understanding regarding spiritual agents, both good and evil? How does your past understanding impact your prayer life?

2. How has the fear of evil impacting you, or the ones you love, shaped you?

3. Throughout the Gospels we see Jesus confronting evil. How do you think he desires to confront personal evil through his people today?

4. Seeing evil societal structures that oppress and harm sometimes overwhelm us to the point that we wonder if we have any hope for change. How might God desire for you to further pray and act as a result of such evils?

5. When pondering or meditating on evil in the world, we must remember that God is not the author of evil (see chapter 1). How might understanding that Jesus is in the process of "making all things new" and "putting everything under his feet" bring you peace and hope?

6

Surrounded by God

Lord, thank you for the food before us,
the family and friends beside us,
and the love between us. Amen.

Growing up in low-church environments afforded me the opportunity to hear life-transforming stories from ordinary lay Christians. From an early age, I heard church and Christian camp testimonies that rivaled Paul's dramatic experience on the road to Damascus. Deliverance from sin, healing from sickness, and freedom from addictions were all a part of the gospel message.

Today I carry a great appreciation for how I was formed to expect God's transformative presence in corporate worship. I am also thankful for being taught that God seeks to touch the whole human person, including minds, bodies, and emotions. Nevertheless, I now see how spiritual passion can skew the way we view God's involvement with his creation and creatures.

To use an example from my childhood, it was not unusual for me to hear a church member remark how refreshing it was that "God showed up" in our gathering that day. For these Christians, God's "showing up" was measured by the intensity of the preaching, the level of enthusiasm in worship, and how long the altar calls lasted. This overly subjective understanding of God's presence is a symptom of what the Eastern Orthodox priest Father Stephen Freeman has called the "two-storey universe" view of reality.

According to Fr. Freeman, this view envisions the world as a two-storey house:

> We live here on earth, the first floor, where things are simply things and everything operates according to normal, natural laws, while God lives in heaven, upstairs, and is largely removed from the storey in which we live. To effect anything here, God must interrupt the laws of nature and perform a miracle.

This vision of reality—which is widespread among contemporary Christians—creates a significant gulf between the dwelling place of God and the area in which daily life occurs. Life is necessarily compartmentalized between "sacred" and "secular" realms. As such, there is the realm "above us" where God dwells and then there is the realm where we dwell and experience everyday affairs. On occasion, God may reach down to do something "supernatural," but otherwise we find ourselves living within the "natural" realm of things. As a result, God is mostly absent from everyday affairs until he decides or is persuaded to become involved in the common matters of life. It is thought, then, that God is to be found on life's mountaintops, but not on life's plains and valleys.

In this split universe, prayer becomes especially problematic. Unanswered prayers become requests that "didn't get beyond the ceiling." The world of the first floor becomes a place where God is mostly missing. Internalizing these ideas, we attempt to live the Christian life without our life united to God's life. And as a result, we end up living a secularized and independent life outside of God.

*

Despite being a children's prayer, embedded within this short petition is a grand vision of reality—one that is much more theologically and biblically robust than the "two-storey universe" view. This prayer offers an alternative way of seeing things in which God is involved in and present everywhere. As our prayer declares, the Lord is "before," "beside," and "between" us. More specifically, in the words of this petition, God is responsible for our sustenance, relationships, and overall intimacy with God and others. He is the constant presence before, beside, and between us. Rather than God being merely above us, this prayer asserts that he is all around us. And this is exactly right.

Consider Psalm 139:7–10:

> Where can I go from your spirit?
> Or where can I flee from your presence?
> If I ascend to heaven, you are there;
> if I make my bed in Sheol, you are there.
> If I take the wings of the morning
> and settle at the farthest limits of the sea,
> even there your hand shall lead me,
> and your right hand shall hold me fast.

For the psalmist, there is no sacred-secular split. The Spirit of God's presence can be known in and through all things.

For too long in Christian circles, God has seemed too distant—too uninvolved in the world. Perhaps this is one reason why some Christians who have deconstructed their faith have found themselves drawn to some form of pantheism—such views that proclaim either that the earth is in some way sacred or that "all is one."

However, there is a better way of viewing the world than adopting *either* the two-storey universe view *or* some form of pantheism. Rather than overemphasizing God's transcendence (otherworldliness) at the expense of God's immanence (this-worldliness) or vice versa, we would be wise to consider that because God is infinite, God transcends the opposition between the two. To put it another way, God is both completely other than his creation all the while being completely embedded within it. God is beyond it *and* intertwined within it. Early Christian theologian John of Damascus (676–749) says exactly this when he states that God "fills all things with His essence . . . but in His power the world does not contain Him." Or as the contemporary English Eastern Orthodox theologian Kallistos Ware has stated, "Our primary image should be that of indwelling. Above and beyond creation, God is also true inwardness, its 'within.'"

What might all this imply?

This suggests that God is indeed infinite and almighty yet all the while being indescribably accessible, even closer than our breath. This means that we cannot separate our lives into two separate realms—"now he's here, now he's not." Instead, God is everywhere present, filling all things.

*

But what about the "us" in this prayer? "Lord, thank you for the food before us, the family and friends beside us, and the love between us." Clearly this children's prayer is not meant to be prayed individually, but corporately. In this tiny prayer, the word "us" shows up three times. So *who* is this "us"? Considering the corporate nature of this Christian prayer, we have to assume this prayer is most appropriately prayed by a group of Christians—the church. This is what the church has always proclaimed: whatever gifts we have, they are from God, whether it be food, people, or something else.

Further, the way God often meets those needs offered in prayer is through the others praying this prayer with us. In other words, often a person in the church holds the answer to the prayer of another around him or her. We see this at the beginning of the church when the early Christian community "were together and had all things in common" (Acts 2:44). How can we pray for someone without also prayerfully acting on their behalf? Or as the biblical writer John declares, "How does God's love abide in anyone who has the world's goods and sees a brother or sister in need and yet refuses help?" (1 John 3:17).

This prayer, then, hints at the nature of the church: a holy *interdependence*. Though this is something we struggle with greatly in much of Western Christianity, living interdependently with one another is considered the biblical norm. Because our society views the person as a self-sufficient or private individual, the church is, by default, seen as a voluntary fellowship. God's community is largely thought to be a group that one may choose to join as long as it meets one's needs and serves one's purposes. As a result, faith is a private matter and is not essentially bound up with others.

This way of thinking, however, is counter to the ways the New Testament writers speak of the church. There are many different images and metaphors used: "the body of Christ" (1 Cor 12:27), "the salt of the earth" (Matt 5:13), "branches of the vine" (John 15:5), "the field of God," "the building of God" (1 Cor 3:9), "God's temple" (1 Cor 3:16), "the bride of Christ" (Eph 5:23–32), "God's own people" (1 Pet 2:9), a "new Jerusalem" (Rev 21:2), and "the household of God" (Eph 2:19). Noticeably, the New Testament authors used collective and mutual images to describe the people of God.

This prayer, then, rightfully pushes us from a privatized form of faith to a more communally oriented one.

However, Dietrich Bonhoeffer wisely warns us of the dangers of rushing into trying to realize this with our own ideas of what true Christian community should look like:

> Every human idealized image that is brought into the Christian community is a hindrance to genuine community and must be broken up so that genuine community can survive. Those who love their dream of a Christian community more than the Christian community itself become destroyers of that Christian community even though their personal intentions may be ever so honest, earnest, and sacrificial. God hates this wishful dreaming because it makes the dreamer proud and pretentious. Those who dream of his idealized community demand that it be fulfilled by God, by others, and by themselves.

Bonhoeffer helps us get to an important truth about the Christian community: rightfully understood, it is not an imagined ideal, but a divine reality. It is not built on nostalgia or emotion, but true spiritual love. Idealistic visions of the church are bound to fail. They are overly emotional and selfish in nature. This is why God calls us toward living in community, offering spiritual love that can only come from Jesus Christ. It does not serve our own purposes, but only serves his. This is the only kind of love that can make a brother or sister of an enemy.

But what does it mean to become Christ's children? How is this familial metaphor in Scripture best understood?

The apostle Paul declares that those in Christ are a part of God's family (Eph 2:19). This truth is foreshadowed on the cross by Jesus telling John that Mary was now his mother (John 19:27). Here, even prior to his resurrection, Jesus is pointing to this reality: being a part of Christ means we are a part of his household. Being joined to him means we are also uniquely joined to others. Christ is bringing in people to become a new kind of people.

Nevertheless, Jesus does not disregard blood relationships. Some have mistakenly read Jesus' seemingly "harsh" sayings regarding blood relatives (Matt 10:34–39; Luke 14:25–25) outside of the overall framework of Jesus' creation of the spiritual family, with devastating results. Jesus is not calling us toward radical separatism. He is not negating the apostle Paul's admonishment that caring for family is crucial to being a Christian (1 Tim 5:8). If loving your neighbor must broaden to include even enemies, how could this same command now exclude one's family? Undoubtedly these sayings are examples of Jesus utilizing rhetorical hyperbole to underscore the significance of his point about family life in his kingdom: love for blood relatives should not cause us to neglect the spiritual family of Christ: "Whoever loves father or mother more than me is not worthy of me" (Matt 10:37).

The purpose of God creating a new family in Christ is for the healing of *all* people. This is a community where we are called to love and be loved, both by God and others. And what makes us "friends and family" in God's kingdom, as the prayer puts, is the "food between us"—the bread of life, Jesus Christ (John 6:35).

And Jesus is clear: to be a part of his family means that we love one another with the same kind of love that we have received from him (John 13:34). From a Christian standpoint, any love that lasts comes from God, considering God *is* love (1 John 4:8). Love is not a quality or an attribute of God. Instead, love—that is, the love of which the Bible speaks—is the very nature of God. Our prayer's reference to the "love between us," then, must be the kind of love that originates in God's life and is poured out for others. This is why Jesus told his disciples that people *will know* whether or not they belong to him depending on how well they *love* one another (John 13:35). He has given us love for it to be shared. He surrounds and indwells his people, empowering them to love as he loves.

*

Though I once envisioned God's activity best demonstrated through expressive church gatherings, I now see that the best evidence of God's activity can be found in the most mundane acts of love. In the apostle Paul's words (1 Cor 13:1-3),

> If I speak in the tongues of mortals and of angels, but do not have love, I am a noisy gong or a clanging cymbal. And if I have prophetic powers, and understand all mysteries and all knowledge, and if I have all faith, so as to remove mountains, but do not have love, I am nothing. If I give away all my possessions, and if I hand over my body so that I may boast, but do not have love, I gain nothing.

While I still wholeheartedly believe that God showcases his power in public gatherings just as he did at Pentecost with the early disciples, I also believe that we see God just as present with Paul in prison in Acts 28 as he was with the early disciples in Acts 2.

If we are going to move into maturity in Christ, we must deconstruct our tendencies to exile God from our daily lives. We must approach the ordinary with expectation and awe. We must grow in appreciation for the objective presence of God found in the church, its preaching, and its sacraments. We must deny the inclination to divide up our lives into "secular" and "sacred" spheres. And we must reconstruct our vision of the world to see God active everywhere, at all times. In Christ Jesus, God is everlastingly with us. As Jürgen Moltmann explains:

> Is God . . . present in everything, everywhere, and at all times, in just the same way? No, there are godforsaken

spaces and situations, there are godless powers. But in the crucified Jesus, God is present even in godforsaken spaces and situations, and in Jesus Christ, the risen and exalted Lord, the godless powers have lost their power. In Christ God is omnipresent, and through him God will be "all in all" (1 Cor 15:28).

For Reflection or Discussion

As you pray this children's prayer in light of this chapter, consider reflecting on and/or discussing the following questions:

1. Do you identify with the "two-storey universe" view? How could this view impact your approach to God and limit your ability to "see God" in the seemingly mundane affairs of life?

2. How can the notion that God is all around you, closer than your next breath, alter the way you go through your day? (How you view your surroundings, interactions, pains, losses, joys, etc.?)

3. When we view the church in an idealized way, we will be disappointed and potentially place unrealistic expectations on others. How will meditating upon and embracing the following quote bring freedom to you as well as others: "[the church] does not serve our own purposes, but only serves his"?

4. Think of, or share a time, when someone was the answer to your prayer.

5. Ponder this quote, "He has given us love for it to be shared. He surrounds and indwells his people, empowering them to love as he loves." Is there someone with whom you are distant or estranged, that God would have you seek out in love?

Postscript: What Next?

IF I can offer a final word to you, my reader, it is this: do not stop at deconstructing your faith—move also toward reconstructing it, *with God and others*. Faithful reconstruction, I believe, requires being honest and prayerful before God, while being open to the insight of wise and trustworthy guides to assist us.

In my view, spiritual and theological deconstruction is sometimes quite necessary. However, I also believe that in order to arrive at belief that is good, beautiful, and true, we need spiritual and theological directors, speaking from within our own context—lest we fail to take our cultural/social setting seriously—and also speaking from outside our own context—lest we fail to adequately identify our cultural/social blind spots.

As I stated from the onset, my principal aim is for readers to take up childlike prayers as acts of faith to see how this might open new ways of understanding specific issues related to Christian faith. Admittedly, my use of children's prayers limited the topics I was able to address, despite the fact that these prayers were crucial to my overall purpose. Even so, this contributed to a possible gap in the book: leaving some important and relevant issues unexplored that are often associated with deconstruction in the Western church, such as the topics of hell, LGBTQI+, and politics, among others.

Despite leaving several crucial issues unexamined, my hope is that these meditations are able illustrate ways of reconstructing prayerful thinking and living. More specifically, I hope that these

Postscript: What Next?

reflections open fresh means of reconceiving Christian belief and living that are culturally and socially engaged while remaining rooted in biblical revelation and the Christian tradition.

It is my hope, then, that you will be able to discern further outlines for your own spiritual and theological reconstruction as a result of this book. I also pray that these reflections have inspired some to consider new angles and perspectives on the issues addressed, while perhaps also encouraging and motivating others to move beyond merely deconstructing their faith toward reconstructing it.

Ultimately, my desire is that you become *maturely dependent* upon God, finding yourself loving God and others more loyally and passionately than before.

Works Cited

Basil of Caesarea. *Hexaemeron*, 2.8. https://www.newadvent.org/fathers/32012.htm.

Blake, William. *The Complete Poetry and Prose of William Blake*. Edited by David V. Erdman. New York: Anchor, 1988.

Bloesch, Donald. *The Last Things: Resurrection, Judgment, Glory*. Downers Grove, IL: IVP Academic, 2004.

Bonhoeffer, Dietrich. *The Collected Sermons of Dietrich Bonhoeffer: Volume 2*. Edited by Victoria J. Barnett. Minneapolis: Fortress, 2017.

———. *Life Together*. San Francisco: Harper Collins, 1978.

Brother Lawrence. *The Practice of the Presence of God*. Old Tappan, NJ: Revell, 1958.

Brunner, Emil. *Dogmatics*. Vol. 1, *The Christian Doctrine of God*. Translated by Olive Wyon. Originally 1949. Eugene, OR: Wipf and Stock, 2014.

———. *Dogmatics*. Vol. 3. *The Christian Doctrine of the Church, Faith, and the Consummation*. Translated by David Cairns with T. H. L. Parker. Originally 1960. Eugene OR: Wipf and Stock, 2014.

———. *The Word and the World*. London: Student Christian Movement Press, 1931.

Buytendijk, F. J. J. *Wesenund Sinn des Spiels*. Berlin: Wolff, 1934.

Cassiday, A. M. *Evagrius Ponticus*. London: Routledge, 2006.

Collins, Billy. *Questions about Angels: Poems*. Pittsburgh: University of Pittsburgh Press, 1991.

Cootsona, Greg. *Mere Science and Christian Faith: Bridging the Divide with Emerging Adults*. Downers Grove, IL: InterVarsity, 2018.

Crockett, Daniel. "Nature Connection Will Be the Next Big Human Trend." *Huffington Post*, August 22, 2014. https://www.huffingtonpost.co.uk/daniel-crockett/nature-connection-will-be-the-next-big-human-trend_b_5698267.html.

Ehrman, Bart. *God's Problem: How the Bible Fails to Answer Our Most Important Question—Why We Suffer*. New York: HarperOne, 2009.

Evagrius Ponticus, *On Prayer* 61. In *Evagrius Ponticus*, edited and translated by A. M. Casiday. 1st ed. New York: Routledge, 2006.

Works Cited

Fergusson, David. *The Providence of God: A Polyphonic Approach*. Cambridge: Cambridge University Press, 2019.

Foster, Richard. *Prayer: Finding the Heart's True Home*. New York: HarperOne, 2002.

Freeman, Stephen. *Everywhere Present: Christianity in a One-Storey Universe*. Chesteron: Ancient Faith, 2011.

Gregory of Nyssa. *The Great Catechism* 26. https://www.newadvent.org/fathers/2908.htm.

Grenz, Stanley. *Theology for the Community of God*. Grand Rapids: Eerdmans, 1994.

Hart, David Bentley. *The Doors of the Sea: Where Was God in the Tsunami?* Grand Rapids: Eerdmans, 2005.

Irenaeus of Lyons. *Against Heresies* V.XXI. https://newadvent.org/fathers 0103521.htm.

Jenson, Robert. *Systematic Theology*. Vol .1, *The Triune God*. New York: Oxford University Press, 1999.

John Cassian. *The Conferences*. Translated by Boniface Ramsey. New York: Paulist, 1997.

John of Damascus. "Orthodox Faith," 1.13. https://newadvent.org/fathers33041.htm.

John Paul II. "Letter of His Holiness Pope John Paul II to the Rev George V. Coyne, S. J., Director of the Vatican Observatory," June 1, 1988. Vatican City: Liberia Editrice Vaticana, 1988. https://www.vatican.va/content/john-paul-ii/en/letters/1988/documents/hf_jp-ii_let_19880601_padre-coyne.html.

Jones, Beth Felker. *Practicing Christian Doctrine: An Introduction to Thinking and Living Theologically*. Grand Rapids: Baker Academic, 2014.

Kärkkäinen, Veli-Matti. *Christian Theology in the Pluralistic World: A Global Introduction*. Grand Rapids: Eerdmans, 2019.

———. *The End of All Things Is at Hand: A Christian Eschatology in Conversation with Science and Islam*. Eugene, OR: Cascade, 2022.

———. *Trinity and Revelation*. Grand Rapids: Eerdmans, 2014.

Knott, Kip. *Tragedy, Ecstasy, Doom, and So On: Poems*. American Fork, UT: Kelsay, 2020.

Leibovich, Mark. "Larry King Is Preparing for the Final Cancellation." *New York Times*, August 26, 2015. https://www.nytimes.com/2015/08/30/magazine/larry-king-is-preparing-for-the-final-cancellation.html.

Lewis, C. S. *Present Concerns: Journalistic Essays*. New York: HarperCollins, 2017.

———. *The Screwtape Letters*. New York: HarperCollins, 1996.

Lossky, Vladimir. *In the Image and Likeness of God*. New York: Saint Vladimir's Seminary Press, 1974.

McGrath, Alister. "Augustine's Origin of Species: How the Great Theologian Might Weigh in on the Darwin Debate." In *The Origins Debate: Evangelical Perspectives on Creation, Evolution, and Intelligent Design*, edited by the editors at *Christianity Today*, 25–29. Carol Stream, IL: Christianity Today, 2012.

———. "On Public Life, Science, Interreligious Dialogue." In *Letters to a Young Theologian*, edited by Henco van der Westhuizen, 15–20. Minneapolis: Fortress, 2022.

Merton, Thomas. *Thoughts in Solitude*. New York: Farrar, Straus and Cudahy, 1958.

Migliore, Daniel. *Faith Seeking Understanding: An Introduction to Christian Theology*. Grand Rapids: Eerdmans, 2004.

Moltmann, Jürgen. "On Ways to Theology." In *Letters to a Young Theologian*, edited by Henco van der Westhuizen, 15–20. Minneapolis: Fortress, 2022.

———. *The Crucified God*. Translated by R. A. Wilson. Minneapolis: Fortress, 1993.

———, ed. *How I Have Changed: Reflections on Thirty Years of Theology*. Translated by John Bowden. Harrisburg, PA: Trinity Press International, 1997.

———. *The Living God and the Fullness of Life*. Translated by Margaret Kohl. Louisville: Westminster John Knox, 2015.

Murray, Andrew. *Abiding in Christ*. Grand Rapids: Bethany House, 2003.

———. *Living a Prayerful Life*. Grand Rapids: Bethany House, 2002.

Nkansah-Obrempong, Jas. "Angels." In *Global Dictionary of Theology*, edited by William A. Dyrness and Veli-Matti Kärkkäinen, 35–39. Downers Grove, IL: InterVarsity, 2008.

Nouwen, Henri. *A Cry for Mercy: Prayers from the Genesee*. New York: Doubleday, 1981.

Origen. *On First Principles*, 2.9.1. In *Origen: On First Principles,* translated by John Behr. Oxford: Oxford University Press, 2019.

Pinnock, Clark. *Flame of Love: A Theology of the Holy Spirit*. Downers Grove, IL: InterVarsity, 1996.

Polkinghorne, John. *Questions of Truth: Fifty-one Responses to Questions about God, Science, and Belief*. Louisville: Westminster John Knox, 2009.

Rahner, Karl. *Foundations of Christian Faith*. New York: Herder & Herder, 1982.

Ramm, Bernard. "Angels." In *Basic Christian Doctrines*, edited by Carl F. H. Henry, 60–66. New York: Holt, Rinehart and Winston, 1962.

Schmemann, Alexander. *For the Life of the World: Sacraments and Orthodoxy*. New York: Saint Vladimir's Seminary Press, 1963.

Smith, Gordon T. *A Holy Meal: The Lord's Supper in the Life of the Church*. Grand Rapids: Baker, 2005.

Swoboda, A. J. *After Doubt: How to Question Your Faith Without Losing It*. Grand Rapids: Brazos, 2021.

Tertullian. *On Prayer*, VI. htttps://www.newadvent.org/fathers/0322.htm.

Thomas, R. S. *R. S. Thomas: Poems*. London: Phoenix Poetry, 2002.

Tomberlin, Daniel. *An Undeconstructed Pentecostal: Reflections, Articles, and Sermons*. Cleveland, TN: Independently Published, 2021.

Works Cited

Ware, Kallistos. "God Immanent Yet Transcendent: The Divine Energies According to Saint Gregory Palamas." In *In Whom We Live and Move and Have Our Being: Panentheistic Reflections on God's Presence in a Scientific World*, edited by Philip Clayton and Arthur Peacocke, 157–68. Grand Rapids: Eerdmans, 2014.

Wesley, John. *Letter to Miss March (June 9, 1775)*. In *The Letters of John Wesley Volume 6*, edited by John Telford, 153–54. London: Epworth, 1931.

Westermann, Claus. *God's Angels Need no Wings*. Minneapolis: Fortress, 1979.

Williams, Rowan. *Being Christian: Baptism, Bible, Eucharist, Prayer*. Grand Rapids: Eerdmans, 2014.

Wright, N. T. *Surprised by Scripture: Engaging Contemporary Issues*. New York: HarperOne, 2015.

Wright, Steve. "The Future of Angelogy." *Faith and Theology Blog*. June 24, 2015. https://www.faith-theology.com/2015/06/the-future-of-angelology.html